ROAD TRIP USA

Atlantic Coast

JAMIE JENSEN

AVALON
TRAVEL

Contents

Atlantic Coast

Starting at the Statue of Liberty and winding up at free-wheeling Key West, these almost 2,000 miles of roadway run within earshot—if not sight— of the Atlantic Ocean.

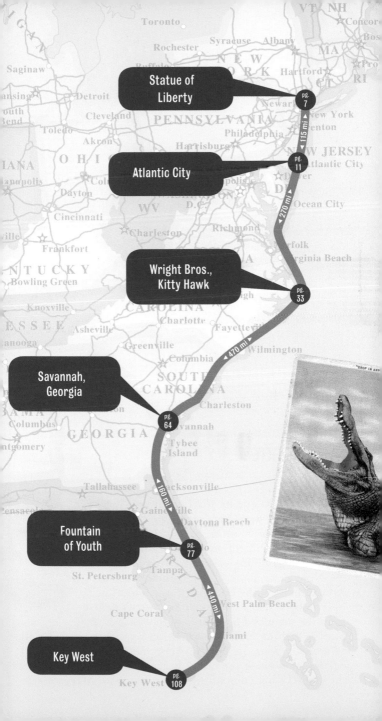

Statue of Liberty — pg. 7

115 mi

Atlantic City — pg. 11

270 mi

Wright Bros., Kitty Hawk — pg. 33

470 mi

Savannah, Georgia — pg. 64

160 mi

Fountain of Youth — pg. 77

440 mi

Key West — pg. 108

"DROP IN ANY

Between New York City and the Tip of Florida

I f your impressions of the East Coast come from driving along the I-95 corridor through nearly nonstop urban and industrial sprawl, following our Atlantic Coast route will open your eyes to a whole other world. Alternating between wildly differing beach resort areas and lengthy stretches of pristine coastal wilderness, the route runs along almost 2,000 miles of two-lane country roads, within earshot, if not sight, of the Atlantic Ocean almost the entire way. In place of the grimy concrete and soulless netherworld of the Interstate, this route passes through innumerable quirky seaside towns and timeless old fishing villages, interspersed with huge swaths of beaches, wetlands, and woodlands that have hardly changed since the first explorers laid eyes on them four centuries ago.

Starting in the north at that all-American icon, the **Statue of Liberty,** and winding up in the south at free-wheeling **Key West,** this route truly offers something for everyone. Those searching for photogenic lighthouses or beachcombing solitude will love the undeveloped and usually deserted strands that stretch for miles

NEW JERSEY

Being so close to New York and Philadelphia, it's not surprising that New Jersey has among the busiest and most densely developed stretches of coastline in the country. It *is* surprising, however, that beyond the boardwalk amusements and flashy gambling casinos of **Atlantic City,** the New Jersey shore offers a whole lot more. As with most of the East Coast, the "shoreline" is actually a series of barrier islands separated from the mainland by wildlife-rich estuaries; these provide fishing and bird-watching opportunities, as well as a break from the ceaseless commercial and residential development along the ocean beaches. Bustling in summer, these beachfront communities—starting with **Margate** near

along the low-lying islands that make up most of the coast, much of which, as at **Assateague Island** or **Cape Hatteras,** has been protected as national seashore parks. In contrast, the many beach resorts that dot the in-between areas vary from the grand Victorian charms of Cape May to the funky old Coney Island–style attractions of **Ocean City, Maryland,** and **Myrtle Beach, South Carolina,** with their boardwalks full of roller coasters, wax museums, and saltwater taffy stands. And let's not forget the glitzy casino resorts of **Atlantic City.**

Alongside the contemporary attractions are many evocative historic sites, including such unique places as **Roanoke Island, North Carolina,** where the first English-speaking colony in North America vanished without a trace in 1587. Lying south of the Mason-Dixon Line for almost all of its length, the route also visits many important Civil War sites, including **Fort Sumter,** where the first shots were fired, and the vital naval battlegrounds at **Hampton Roads** at the mouth of Chesapeake Bay. Midway along, we also pass one of the key sites of modern history: the windy sand dunes at **Kitty Hawk** where the Wright Brothers first proved that humans could fly.

Though this Atlantic Coast route will bring you to many well-known sights, its real attraction is the traveling, stopping off for fried chicken or barbecue at one of the hundreds of roadside stands, watching the shrimp boats pull into a sleepy dock and unload their day's catch, or simply chatting with locals at the general store or post office in a town that may not even be on the map.

Atlantic City, and running south through vibrant **Wildwood** before winding up at the dainty Victorian-era beach resort of **Cape May**—offer something for everyone, all within a 150-mile stretch of shoreline.

The Statue of Liberty

Raising her lamp beside New York City's immense harbor, the **Statue of Liberty** is one of the most vivid emblems of America. Despite the fact she is French, given to the American people to celebrate the 100th anniversary of the Declaration of Independence, the statue has come to symbolize the Land of the Free and the Home of the Brave. Its spirit has long been evoked by the poem Emma Lazarus wrote in 1883 to help raise funds for installing the Statue of Liberty. Called "The New Colossus," the poem ends with these famous words:

New York City

Some people avoid New York City like the plague, but more than eight million others can't bear to leave the glorious buzzing mosaic that makes New York unique in the world. Love it or hate it, New York is New York, and this great metropolis is undeniably the capital of the capitalist world, with some of the best museums, the best shops, the best sights, and the best restaurants in the world.

There's not much point in our recommending a select few of New York's huge spectrum of attractions, so we'll get straight to offering some practical help. For drivers, to whom all roads must seem to converge upon—and become gridlocked in—New York City, if you value your sanity and your shock absorbers park your car in a long-term lot (not on the streets; city parking regulations are arcane and the fines huge) and walk or take public transportation. New York's subway system, one of the most extensive in the world, is relatively safe and usually the fastest way to get around town; it's also inexpensive ($2.25 per ride, or $8 a day, payable via electronic Metrocard). City buses are generally slower, but you see more of the sights. Taxis are ubiquitous—except when you want one.

The key to a successful visit to New York City is finding a place to stay. Ideally, you'll have an expense account, a friend, or a rich aunt, but lacking that, here are a few suggestions, most in the low-to-moderate range. It's hard to beat the **Holiday Inn Soho** ($225 and up; 138 Lafayette St.; 212/966-8898) for convenience, as it's equidistant from Chinatown, Little Italy, SoHo, and TriBeCa. For families, another good option is the **Embassy Suites** ($299 and up; 102 North End Ave.; 212/945-0100) at Battery Park City, with views of the Statue of Liberty. The least expensive place in town is the very large and popular **HI-New York Hostel** (891 Amsterdam Ave.; 212/932-2300), on the Upper West Side at 103rd Street, with private rooms (around $75) plus dorm beds for less than $29 a night. One of the many fabulous hotels in New York City is the small, stylish, and recently renovated Ian Shrager hotel, **Morgans** ($250 and up; 237 Madison Ave.; 212/686-0300).

Eating out is another way to blow a lot of money very quickly, but there are some great places where you can get both a good

meal and a feel for New York without going bankrupt. One such place is **Katz's Delicatessen** (205 E. Houston St.; 212/254-2246), a Lower East Side landmark that's been serving up huge sandwiches (including great pastrami) since 1888. (For movie buffs, Katz's is where Meg Ryan did her famous fake-orgasm scene in *When Harry Met Sally.*) And if you like diners, check out the **Star on 18** (128 10th Ave.; 212/366-0994), at 18th Street in the Chelsea neighborhood—then take a leisurely walk on the magical High Line, a long-abandoned rail line recently reborn as a stylish pedestrian path, 20 feet above the not-so-mean streets. Another affordable all-American experience can be had at the retro-trendy **Shake Shack,** a high-style burger stand across from the iconic Flatiron Building in Madison Square Park, a leafy oasis off Madison Avenue at East 23rd Street (212/889-6600). On the Upper East Side, between the Metropolitan and Whitney museums, Michelin-starred chef Daniel Boulud serves up exquisitely prepared French bistro fare at his **Cafe Boulud** (20 E. 76th St.; 212/772-2600). The ever-changing menu features a wide variety of traditional favorites and contemporary inventions, available for lunch and dinner at (comparatively) moderate prices. It's very popular, so make reservations as soon as you can.

High Line park, formerly a rail line, now serves as a green pedestrian path.

"Keep ancient lands, your storied pomp!" cries she
With silent lips. "Give me your tired, your poor,
Your huddled masses yearning to breathe free,
The wretched refuse of your teeming shore.
Send these, the homeless, tempest-tost to me,
I lift my lamp beside the golden door!"

Inspired by the end of slavery following the Civil War, the Statue of Liberty took nearly 20 years to complete. Lady Liberty was sculpted in France, then the 300-plus pieces were put in crates and shipped across the ocean. The statue is just over 150 feet tall, but including her 150-foot stone pedestal, it was the tallest building in New York when dedicated in 1886.

The Statue of Liberty sits on a 12-acre island and can be visited by ferry only (daily; $13; 877/LADY-TIX). It's about a mile from Manhattan, but much easier to reach from **Liberty State Park** in Jersey City, off New Jersey Turnpike exit 14B. So long as you start your trip before 2 PM, both ferry routes also visit Ellis Island, where some 12 million immigrants entered the United States. There is no admission fee for the Statue of Liberty or Ellis Island, but if you want to climb up onto Lady Liberty's pedestal you need a free, time-stamped Monument Pass, which you can get when you buy your ferry tickets.

All pass-holders can explore the base of the Statue of Liberty and gaze up inside her hollow shell, but access up into the very small viewing area in the crown on her head requires special tickets ($3 extra) and a climb up more than 350 steps. Her torch has been off-limits since 1916. In the security-conscious environment, the welcoming sentiments expressed in the Lazarus poem can seem quite sharply ironic, and sadly, the experience of visiting the statue can end up having more to do with restrictions and limitations than it does with grand concepts like "Liberty."

The New Jersey Shore

The northernmost stretches of the New Jersey shore are not exactly appealing, and visitors bound for the beaches

and vacation spots farther south turn a blind eye to the industrial blight. From **Perth Amboy** (Vaseline) to **Asbury Park** (Bruce Springsteen), the region has given the world many distinctive products, and there are a couple of intriguing Victorian-era resorts like **Spring Lake** and **Avon-by-the-Sea,** but to be honest, the attractions increase the farther south you go.

The middle stretch of the Jersey shore is actually the quietest, with the million-acre **Pinelands National Preserve** (daily; free; 609/894-7300) covering the inland area with forest and wetlands, and the coastal **Long Beach Island** dotted with sleepy little fishing and retirement communities. The biggest sight hereabouts is at the northern tip of the island: **Barnegat Lighthouse** (daily; free; 609/494-2016), "Old Barney," whose image appears on personalized New Jersey license plates.

Atlantic City

Midway along the Jersey Shore, the world-famous beach resort of **Atlantic City** (pop. 39,558) has ridden the ups and downs of history. Home of the world's oldest beachfront boardwalk and the first pleasure pier,

Atlantic City also spawned the picture postcard and the Miss America beauty contest. Perhaps most significant of all, the street names for Monopoly were taken from Atlantic City, although the city's layout bears little resemblance to the board game (and there's no "Get Out of Jail Free" card, either).

Atlantic City reached its peak at the turn of the 20th century, when thousands of city-dwellers flocked here from New York and Philadelphia each weekend. Later on, as automobiles and airplanes brought better beaches and more exotic locales within reach, Atlantic City went into a half century of decline until **gambling** was legalized in the 1970s and millions of dollars flowed into the local economy from speculating real-estate developers like Donald Trump, whose name is emblazoned on a number of towering resort hotels. These days, the Boardwalk of Atlantic

sunset on the beach, Atlantic City

City has been transformed from a derelict relic into a glitzy gambling resort, attracting some 30 million annual visitors and millions of dollars daily to its casinos. It's no Las Vegas, and the population is still comparatively poor and shrinking, but the clattering of slot machines and the buzz of the craps tables continues 24 hours a day year-round.

To enjoy a day on the sands at many of New Jersey's beaches, you need to buy (and wear) a beach badge, which costs around $2 a day and is available at local tourist offices, shops, and fast-food stands.

The **Boardwalk,** backed by a wall of 25-story casino/hotels, is still the main focus of Atlantic City, running along the beach for over two miles. Few of the remaining pleasure piers offer much of interest, and only the rebuilt **Steel Pier,** located opposite Trump's Taj Mahal, holds the traditional seaside rides

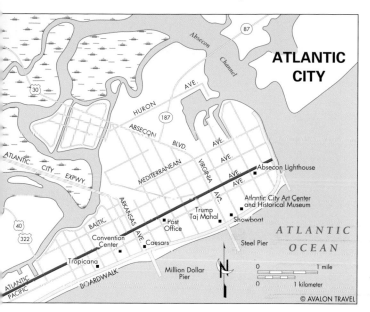

and arcade games, plus a sometimes-lively branch of the House of Blues nightclub chain.

Besides constituting Atlantic City's main attractions, the casinos hold most of the places to eat, apart from the dozens of fast-food stands along the Boardwalk. That said, a couple of old favorites stand out from the seedy crowd of ramshackle businesses that fill the nearby streets. One is the birthplace of the "submarine" sandwich, the chrome **White House Sub Shop** (2301 Arctic Ave.; 609/345-1564), open until midnight every day.

Boardwalk at Atlantic City

A block away, but at the other end of the aesthetic and budgetary spectrum, is **Dock's Oyster House** (2405 Atlantic Ave.; 609/345-0092), a white-linen, dinner-only restaurant that's been serving great seafood since 1897. Along with a number of national chains, the casinos also control accommodation options—expect to pay upwards of $100 a night, though off-peak bargains can be found.

Lucy the Elephant

Margate: Lucy the Elephant

Immediately south of Atlantic City, tidy **Margate** (pop. 8524) fans out along the shore, its solidly suburban streets lined by grand houses. Margate utterly lacks the reckless seaside qualities of its larger neighbor but does include one classic remnant of the Jersey shore's glory days: **Lucy the Elephant** (daily in summer, limited hours rest of the year; $7; 9200 Atlantic Ave.; 609/823-6473). The six-story wood-and-tin pachyderm, a curiosity built by a Philadelphia real-estate speculator in the 1880s to draw customers to his newly laid-out community, looms over the beach. The landmark architectural folly was used around the turn of the 20th century as a tavern and now holds a small museum of local history. Visitors walk through the museum on the way up to an observation deck, which is disguised as a canopied seat on Lucy's back.

Saved from demolition and restored by community efforts in the 1970s, Lucy is ever in need of repair, kept alive by tour monies, donations, and sales of Lucy souvenirs in the small gift shop.

Ocean Drive: Ocean City and Stone Harbor

A series of local roads collectively known as **Ocean Drive** runs along the south Jersey coast, passing through a number of family-oriented beach resorts, starting at Ocean City, "The Greatest Family Resort for a Vacation, or a Lifetime," 10 miles south of Atlantic City. **Ocean City** (pop. 14,699) was founded as a religious retreat in the late 1870s and hasn't strayed far from its roots: Every summer morning (at 9:20 AM, on the dot), life on the Boardwalk promenade comes to a standstill as "The Star-Spangled Banner" blares out from loudspeakers and the American flag is raised at the beachfront amusement park. Located at 6th Street, and known as **Gillian's Wonderland Pier** (daily in summer, weekends only spring and fall; free admission, fee per ride; 609/399-7082), this old-time funfair has over 30 rides, including a giant Ferris wheel and a 1920s carousel. A block south, you can cool off on a hot summer's day at **Gillian's Island** water park.

Vacation homes, marinas, miniature golf courses, and a pair of toll bridges mark Ocean Drive for the next 20 miles. At **Stone Harbor,** five miles north of Wildwood, the **Wetlands Institute** (daily in summer, Tues.–Sat. rest of year; $8; 1075 Stone Harbor Blvd.; 609/368-1211) is one of the best places to experience the abundant natural life of the New Jersey shore. An observation tower looking over 6,000 acres of saltwater marshland provides excellent bird-watching opportunities, and there's also a museum with a touch-tank and aquarium.

Wildwood

On the Jersey Shore, fun in the sun reaches a peak at raucous **Wildwood,** a trio of interconnected towns housing dozens of nightclubs and New Jersey's biggest beachfront amusement parks. The largest of all, **Mariners Landing** on the pier at Schellenger Avenue, has 35 rides including the largest Ferris wheel on the East Coast. At 25th Street is **Morey's Pier,** which has a miniature golf course that takes you through the history of the New Jersey shore. A little farther south is **Morey's Adventure Pier,** which is home to the Great White, the only wooden roller coaster in the U.S. to be built on a pier. All three of these are owned by the Morey family, prime movers behind Wildwood's retro-rediscovery, and an all-ride, all-pier pass (around $60; 609/522-3900)

is available for a full day's fun. Batting cages, go-karts, and some of the wilder rides are not included in the pass price.

Away from the sands in the low-key downtown district, Wildwood's local history **museum** (free; 3907 Pacific Ave.; 609/523-0277) is worth a look for its one unique feature: the **National Marbles Hall of Fame,** featuring thousands of glass balls and more marble-shooting paraphernalia than you've ever seen. The museum, which hosts the National Marbles Championship every June, also has a fascinating and informative display of postcards documenting the region's recent past.

For many visitors, the best reason to spend time in Wildwood is that the area boasts an extensive collection of 1950s roadside architecture—mainly motel after motel, all sporting exuberant Las Vegas–style neon signs. Many of these motels are closed in the November–May off-season, but in the warmer months you can step back in the past by staying the night in one of these classic "Doo Wop" motels—like the **Mango Motel** (209 E. Spicer Ave.; 609/522-2067) or the renovated **Lollipop Motel** (2301 Atlantic Ave.; 609/729-2800).

Chili dog lovers will want to chow down at **Maui's Dog House** (806 New Jersey Ave.; 609/846-0444), at the north end of town, while other retro-minded visitors will want to stop for a meal at the chrome-and-glass **Pink Cadillac Diner** (3801 Atlantic Ave.; 609/522-8288), a block south of the main pier.

For more details on places to stay and things to do—like October's massive and rowdy **Thunder on the Beach** monster truck rally—contact the **Wildwood visitors center** (3601 Boardwalk; 800/992-9732).

Cape May

A world away from the carnival atmosphere of the Wildwoods, **Cape May,** the oldest and most serene of the New Jersey beach towns, sits at the southern tip of the state. First settled in the early 1600s, Cape May's glory years ran from the 1850s to the 1890s as an upper-crust summer resort, when it rivaled Newport, Rhode Island, as the destination of choice for the power brokers of Philadelphia and New York City.

A few modern motels and miniature golf courses spread along Cape May's broad beaches, while the compact downtown district retains all its overwrought Victorian splendor. Century-old cottages now house cafés, boutiques, and art

Cape May–Lewes Ferry

Running between the tip of the New Jersey shore and the heart of the Delaware coast, the Cape May–Lewes Ferry carries cars and passengers on a relaxing ride across the mouth of Delaware Bay. The trip ranges in cost depending upon day and season (summer weekends being most expensive), from about $30 to $45 each way for a car and one passenger, plus fees for each additional passenger.

the *Cape May*, one of the five boats in the fleet

Schedules change seasonally, with boats leaving about every two hours in summer and every three hours in winter. Crossings take about 90 minutes, and if the seas are calm you can often see porpoises playing in the swells.

For up-to-date times and other information, call 800/643-3779. Reservations ($5 extra) are a very good idea at peak travel times and should be made at least one day in advance.

galleries, and it seems as if every other building has been converted into a quaint B&B. The town's ornate gingerbread mansions were constructed in the aftermath of a disastrous 1878 fire; among the better examples is the elaborate **Emlen Physick House** (1048 Washington St.), eight blocks north of downtown, designed by noted Philadelphia architect Frank Furness. It now houses the nonprofit, preservation-oriented **Mid-Atlantic Center for the Arts** and is open as a museum of late Victorian life (daily in summer, weekends only in winter; $8; 609/884-5404).

Pick up walking-tour maps of some of the town's 600 listed historic buildings and do a taste-test of Cape May's many architecturally magnificent, mostly Victorian-era bed-and-breakfasts. These include the mansard-roofed **Queen Victoria** ($115 and up; 102 Ocean St.; 609/884-8702),and the **Mainstay Inn** ($175 and up; 635 Columbia Ave.; 609/884-8690), which has a spacious veranda opening onto gorgeous gardens. Cape May's oldest and most atmospheric place to stay is the Southern gothic **Chalfonte Hotel** ($89–189; 301 Howard St.; 609/884-8409). What the Chalfonte lacks in TVs and telephones it more than makes up for in hospitality: a bank of front-porch rocking chairs, full breakfasts, and huge, down-home dinners are all included in the rates.

Places to eat, including a dozen or so bakeries, cafés, restaurants, and bars, can be found along the pedestrian-friendly few blocks of Washington Street at the center of town, while the seafood restaurants, naturally enough, are near the marina and ferry terminal on the north edge of town, off US-9. One more great option for a hearty all-American breakfast or a Greek-inflected lunch or dinner: **George's Place,** right downtown on the water (cash only; 301 Beach Ave.; 609/884-6088), is perhaps the most popular place in whole Garden State, with lines snaking out the door.

DELAWARE

Across Delaware Bay from Cape May, the Delaware shore is considerably quieter and more peaceful than New Jersey's. Both shores, originally settled by Scandinavian whalers who established port colonies here in the early 1600s, share a common history. But because the Delaware shore is that much farther from the urban centers, it has been spared the overdevelopment of much of the rest of the coast. Nevertheless, Delaware's statewide population doubles in summer as visitors from Baltimore and Washington, D.C., descend upon its coastal resorts, from historic **Lewes** to lively **Rehoboth Beach** to the untouched sands of **Delaware Seashore State Park,** stretching south to the Maryland border.

Lewes and Cape Henlopen

Sitting at the southern lip of Delaware Bay, **Lewes** is a vacation and sportfishing center that traces its roots back to 1631, when it was settled by the Dutch West India Company as a whaling port. Though this colony lasted only two years, Lewes calls itself the "First Town in the First State," commemorating its history in the false-gabled brick

Zwannendael Museum at the center of town (closed Mon.; free; 102 Kings Hwy.; 302/645-1148). Lewes also harbors huge sand dunes, a fine stretch of beach, and a **campground** with show-ers in 3,000-acre **Cape Henlopen State Park** (302/645-8983), east of town at the mouth of Delaware Bay. Expect relative peace and quiet here, since many visitors, arriving off the Cape May ferry, simply rush through Lewes to the beach resorts farther south.

Zwannendael Museum

Just north of US-9, look out for **Cafe Azafran** (109 W. Market St.; 302/644-4446), a very welcoming, wholesome, and flavorful trans-European café that's open for breakfast, lunch, and dinner, serving good coffee, cold beer, and fine wines along with French cheese, Spanish Serrano ham, Greek olives, and a whole range of regional delicacies.

Rehoboth Beach

Fronting the open Atlantic, **Rehoboth Beach** was found-ed in the 1870s when church groups bought beachfront land, established the town, and extended a railroad line south from Lewes. The high-way frontage along Hwy-1 is over-full of franchise food and factory outlet malls, but the heart of town along Rehoboth Avenue is the place to go. With its summer-only but very lively Sputnik-era **Funland Amusement Park** (302/227-1921, open May–Sept., hours vary), where

Ever wonder what happens to all those pumpkins that don't get bought by Halloween? In Delaware, they end up as fodder for a unique competition, the **Punkin' Chunkin',** in which the hapless gourds get launched hundreds, even thousands of feet through the air by a variety of mechanical devices. Thousands turn out for the event, which is usually held on a farm at Coverdale Crossroads, 30 miles west of Lewes, on the first weekend in November ($9, intersection of Seashore Hwy. and Chaplains Chapel Rd.).

the attractions include bumper cars, a nighttime haunted house, and a tidy boardwalk running along the broad beach, Rehoboth has somehow retained a small-town feel despite the many thousands of bureaucrats and power brokers who descend upon the place during the summer, escaping the sweltering heat of Washington, D.C.

The D.C. connection helps explain the town's profusion of very good (and some very expensive) restaurants. Lining the main drag are casual, kid-friendly places like **Dogfish Head** (320 Rehoboth Ave.; 302/226-2739), which has great food and killer beers in Delaware's oldest microbrewery. More grown-up palates will be drawn to the gourmet places a block south, where the outrageously kitsch **La La Land** (22 Wilmington Ave.; 302/227-3887) fills a pair of old beach houses alongside the eclectic, Mediterranean-inspired and unfailingly yummy **Espuma** (28 Wilmington Ave.; 302/227-4199). There are also the more mainstream delights of **Thrashers French Fries,** and sundry beer-and-burger stands along the boardwalk.

Places to stay include some quaint old B&Bs and a barrage of highway chain motels, plus local ones like the **Beach View** ($70 and up; 6 Wilmington Ave.; 302/227-2999), on the boardwalk.

Delaware Seashore State Park

South from Rehoboth stretches one of the last long stretches of pristine beach on the whole northern East Coast: **Delaware Seashore State Park** (302/227-3071), which contains six miles of open beach with golden-flecked white sand and 2,825 acres of marshland estuary, thronged in season with migrating birds—and bird-watchers (and campers and anglers, too.) The park's many beaches are all easily accessible from beachfront Hwy-1.

The park has camping and nice new cottages (costing $1,800 a week during prime summer season!) and is bookended by a pair of densely developed resort towns: **Dewey Beach** in the north draws a younger, collegiate crowd, while **Bethany Beach** in the south attracts more families.

Near Maryland, the 1858 **Fenwick Island Lighthouse,** on the bay side of Hwy-1 just south of Hwy-54, marks the state border. This lighthouse is a local landmark, but the waist-high white marker in front of it may be more significant: Placed in 1751, it marked the boundary between Maryland and Pennsylvania, of which Delaware was then a part. Showing respect to the colonial proprietors, the more than 250-year-old marker has the Calvert family coat of arms on the Maryland (south) side and William Penn's family crest on the other.

MARYLAND

Maryland, the most oddly shaped of the lower 48 states, shares the broad "DelMarVa" peninsula with Delaware and a small piece of Virginia. The inland area along the eastern shore of Chesapeake Bay, with its many inlets and tributary rivers, is filled with dozens of small colonial-era towns and fishing villages, while the Atlantic Coast is completely taken up by two very different beasts: the gloriously kitschy beach resort of **Ocean City** and the untrammeled wilds of **Assateague Island National Seashore.** Heading inland around Assateague, the highway passes by a number of historic small towns, including **Berlin** and captivating **Snow Hill.**

Ocean City

About the only place left on the entire East Coast that retains the carnival qualities of classic seaside resorts, **Ocean City** (pop. 7,105, swelling to some 400,000 in summer) has by far the best array of old-time funfair attractions in the Mid-Atlantic (well, south of Wildwood, New Jersey, at least). On and around the main pier at the south end of the island, there are enough merry-go-rounds, Ferris wheels, roller coasters (including The Hurricane, which is illustrated with scenes from Ocean City storms

To go along with its great beaches, Ocean City has a radio station, the excellent **WOCM 98.1 FM,** playing classic rock 'n' roll and broadcasting details of Ocean City's nightclub scene.

past), mini-golf courses, haunted houses, and bumper cars to divert a small army. A block inland, **Trimper's Amusements,** which has been operated by the same family for five generations, since the 1890s, has two more roller coasters, plus a Tilt-a-Whirl, a 100-year-old Hershell carousel, and a spooky haunted house. Places like Trimper's, and the sundry batting cages, go-kart tracks, and zip lines, are threatened by rising property values (and property taxes) and increasingly close to becoming extinct, so enjoy them while you can. Trimpers's local rival, Jolly Roger, also runs a big water park and another amusement park at the north end of town, along the bay at 30th Street.

OCEAN CITY

ATLANTIC OCEAN

Isle of Wight Bay

528
BALTIMORE
PHILADELPHIA
9TH ST
7TH ST
5TH ST
3RD ST
1ST ST
BOARDWALK
50
TALBOT
Life Saving Station Museum
AVE
0   .5 mile
0   .5 kilometer
© AVALON TRAVEL

From the pier north, Ocean City stretches for over three miles along a broad, clean, white-sand beach. A wide, part-wooden boardwalk lines the sands, packed with arcades full of video games and a few nearly forgotten old amusements like Skee-Ball and Pokerino, not to mention midway contests—the kind where, for $1 a try, you can win stuffed animals and other prizes by shooting baskets or squirt-

Haunted House at Trimper's Amusements, Ocean City

ing water into clowns' mouths. A ramshackle collection of fortune-tellers, T-shirt stands, and burger-and-beer bars completes the scene, forming a busy gauntlet that is among the nation's liveliest promenades.

On summer weekends, Ocean City becomes

Maryland's second-largest city, and most of the fun is simply in getting caught up in the garish human spectacle of it all, but there are a couple of specific things worth searching out. For the price of a bumper car ride, you can enjoy the quirky collections of the **Life-Saving Station Museum** (daily May–Oct., weekends only in winter; $3), at the south end of the boardwalk, where alongside displays of shipwrecks and bathing suits you can compare and contrast bowls full of sand from 100 different beaches around the world. The museum also marks the starting point for the open-air trams ($3) that run north along the boardwalk for over two miles.

Ocean City Practicalities

Much of Ocean City's charm is decidedly lowbrow, but the food is better than you might expect, with numerous places offering plates full of shrimp and pitchers of beer for under $10, and freshly fried chicken or crab cakes available from boardwalk stands. **Thrashers Fries** are available (no ketchup; salt and vinegar only!) from a number of counters along the boardwalk, and you can top them off with a cone or milk shake from **Dumser's Ice Cream,** which runs a trio of stands at the south end of the boardwalk.

Places to stay are also abundant, though many of the huge concrete towers you see are actually condominiums and not available for overnight stays. In fact, of all the dozen or more grand, older hotels, only the **Atlantic Hotel** ($80 and up;

aerial view of Ocean City

5 Somerset St.; 410/289-9111), on the oceanfront, is still open for business. Modern motels like the **Oceanic** (710 S. Philadelphia St.; 410/289-6494), looking across the inlet to Assateague Island, charge as much as $200 a night for a room that goes for less than $50 off-season.

For help finding lodgings and restaurants, contact the **Ocean City visitors center** (4001 Coastal Hwy.; 410/723-8600 or 800/626-2326), in the Convention Center.

Assateague Island National Seashore

At one time, Assateague Island, the long thin barrier island on which Ocean City sits, stretched in an unbroken line all the way into Virginia. In 1933, a major storm crashed through the sands and created the broad inlet that now divides Ocean City from the near-wilderness of **Assateague Island National Seashore.** One of the few areas of the Atlantic coast protected from commercial development, Assateague Island offers some 37 miles and 10,000 acres of hiking, swimming, camping, canoeing, bicycling, clamming, and bird-watching. Swarms of voracious mosquitoes and a lack of fresh water keep the crowds to a minimum.

To reach the island from Ocean City, follow US-50 west for two miles and turn south on Hwy-611, which loops around Sinexpunt Bay before arriving at the **visitors center** (daily; 410/641-1441). The center has a small aquarium, as well as maps, guides, and up-to-date information about the national seashore.

On the road between Ocean City and Assateague Island, at the junction of US-50 and Hwy-611, the very nice **Wheels of Yesterday** vehicle museum ($5; 410/213-7329) displays more than 30 classic cars and trucks and has a great little gift shop, too.

Berlin and Snow Hill

From Ocean City, the route turns inland around Assateague Island and Chincoteague Bay, following US-50 west for eight miles, then turning south on US-113 through the dark cypress swamps along the Pocomoke River. Just southwest of the US-50/113 junction, the remarkably well-preserved town of **Berlin** offers a look back at a slower-paced era. Redbrick buildings house antiques shops around the 1890s landmark **Atlantic Hotel** ($60 and up; 2 N. Main St.; 410/641-3589), where the rocking chairs along the open-air front porch all but demand that you sit and stay a while. Inside, the very stylish **Drummers Cafe** (open at 11 AM daily) may tempt you to alter your travel plans so you can enjoy the delicious local seafood.

Another 15 miles southwest of Ocean City, detour west from the highway to take a look at the 250-year-old town of **Snow Hill** (pop. 2,409). The **Julia A. Purnell Museum** (Tues.–Sun. Apr.–Oct. only; $2; 208 W. Market St.), housed in an old church, features a range of exhibits tracing Eastern Shore history, including a 200-year-old iron furnace and a one-room schoolhouse. Pick up a walking-tour map of Snow Hill's many significant structures, or if the weather's fine, paddle a canoe or a kayak through the surrounding wild cypress swamps with the **Pocomoke River Canoe Company** (312 N. Washington St.; 410/632-3971), next to the drawbridge.

VIRGINIA

Virginia's Eastern Shore is among the most isolated regions of the country, and its dozens of small towns and villages remain much as they have for centuries. Everything on the Eastern Shore is on a much smaller scale than on the mainland, and the many stands selling fresh corn and tomatoes along the roadside attest to the important role farming plays in the local economy. Although fast-food places, chicken-processing plants, and a couple of modern malls dot US-13, the main route through Virginia's Eastern Shore, the area is still mostly rural and undeveloped, with business loops turning off through the many well-preserved old towns. The numerous historic sites include colonial-era plantations and archaeological remnants of Native American tribes.

The highlight for most visitors is **Chincoteague,** a small commercial and sportfishing port sitting at the entrance to massive Chincoteague National Wildlife Refuge, which faces the Atlantic Coast and offers the only ocean beaches in this part of the state. South of Chincoteague, US-13 runs down the center of the narrow Eastern Shore peninsula, giving access to the Chesapeake Bay waterfront at **Accomac,** then passing through numerous small towns like **Onancock** and **Eastville,** neither of which has changed much since Revolutionary times. Crossing the mouth of the Chesapeake Bay via a 23-mile-long bridge and tunnel brings you to maritime **Norfolk** and the state's main Atlantic resort, **Virginia**

Beach, before the route turns inland and south into North Carolina.

Chincoteague

The drive into **Chincoteague** (pop. 4,317; pronounced "SCHINK-a-teeg"), a low-key fishing village, takes you across miles of glowing gold and blue marshlands through a gauntlet of quirky billboards advertising local motels, restaurants, and sportfishing charters. This mix of natural beauty and tacky tourism aptly reflects the character of the town, which is totally dependent upon summertime visitors but seems to wish that we'd all just leave and let the locals go fishing.

A small bridge along Hwy-175, which runs 10 miles east from US-13, drops you at the heart of town, where casual seafood restaurants line the small wharves that stretch along the bay. For breakfast, head south of town, where the popular **Mr. Baldy's Family Restaurant** (3441 Ridge Rd.; 757/336-1198) serves up hearty meals across from the "pony swim" landing at Black Point. Near here, at the end of Beebe Street just outside the refuge boundary, you can pitch a tent or park an RV at the very pleasant, privately owned **Tom's Cove Campground** (757/336-6498).

In summer, stands selling fresh fruit and vegetables—particularly sweet corn and tomatoes—dot roadsides all over the Eastern Shore.

Among the many places to stay are several nice B&Bs and a handful of standard motels like the friendly and central **Birchwood** ($65 and up; 3650 N. Main St.; 757/336-6133).

wild ponies at Chincoteague National Wildlife Refuge

Chincoteague National Wildlife Refuge

Spreading east of town, the **Chincoteague National Wildlife Refuge** is one of the largest nature preserves along the Atlantic flyway, attracting hundreds of species of birds, including egrets, herons, geese, swans, and snow geese, not

to mention thousands and thousands of migrating ducks. A continuation of the Assateague Island National Seashore across the Maryland border, the refuge contains thousands of acres of marshland, excellent beaches, and a number of hiking and cycling trails. The refuge **visitors center** (daily; 757/336-6577) has detailed information on park activities as well as special exhibits on Chincoteague's famous wild ponies, which can usually be seen from the Woodland Trail that loops south from Beach Road.

The children's story *Misty of Chincoteague* is set in the area and tells how wild ponies—whose ancestors were sent here by English settlers in the late 1600s—are rounded up from the wildlife refuge on Assateague Island for a forced swim across to Chincoteague. The annual roundup, swim, and auction benefits local firefighters and attracts thousands of spectators. The swim takes place the last Wednesday in July, and the auction follows the next day.

Accomac

One of the most photogenic spots on the Eastern Shore, **Accomac** (pop. 547) is centered on an ancient-looking redbrick courthouse, flanked by a series of wooden sheds converted into professional offices. The old library next door dates from the 1780s and was used for years as a debtors' prison; the library, courthouse, and surrounding buildings together make for a great leg-stretch spot, midway along the Eastern Shore. By way of contrast, Accomac is also home to another Eastern Shore landmark: the huge Perdue Chicken processing plant, right along US-13, which produces and packs more than 12 million birds every year.

Onancock and Tangier Island

The picturesque harbor town of **Onancock** (pop. 1,525; pronounced "o-NAN-cock"), on the Chesapeake Bay two miles west of US-13 via Hwy-179, is one of the nicest towns on the Eastern Shore. A short walking tour of over a dozen historical homes and churches begins at perhaps the finest mansion on the Eastern Shore, the **Ker Place** (Tues.–Sat. 11 AM–4 PM; $8; 69 Market St.; 757/787-8012), built in 1799 and now home to the offices and museum of the Eastern Shore of Virginia Historical Society. Another historical curiosity is the 150-year-old Hopkins and Bros. General Store, on the wharf (2 Market St.), which in the past has sold everything from sweet potatoes to postcards—and now serves as a sort of mini welcome center.

A great taste of Onancock life awaits inside the **Corner Bakery** (36 Market St.; 757/787-4520), where great doughnuts and fresh coffee are served up to a mostly local crowd, or in the evening you can catch a flick at Onancock's nifty 1950s movie theater, the **Roseland** (48 Market St.; 757/787-2209). Dinner and nice rooms are available at the **Charlotte Hotel** (7 North St.; 757/787-7400). Finally, back on US-13, the hamlet of Exmoor has one last road-food stop, the **Exmoor Diner.**

Onancock was born and grew up around its natural deep-water harbor, and the town wharf is still the place to catch the seasonal ferry across Chesapeake Bay to **Tangier Island,** an evocative old place where things seem to have hardly changed since colonial times. The few hundred people who live here year-round have a unique and almost indecipherably archaic accent—which some trace back to 17th-century Cornwall, England—and earn their livelihoods catching crabs and the occasional oyster from Chesapeake Bay. Tangier Island is best known for its soft-shell crabs, which are sold all over the eastern United States.

Visiting Tangier Island is easy but takes some advance planning. From mid-April until October, boats leave once a day Tuesday–Saturday from Onancock Wharf (about $25; 757/891/2505); travel time is one hour and 15 minutes each way, leaving around 10 AM and returning around 3 PM This means visitors returning on the ferry have only about two hours on the island, so staying overnight at a homespun B&B like **Shirley's Bay View Inn** (757/891-2396) or **Hilda Crockett's Chesapeake House** (757/891-2331) is about the only way to have any kind of close encounter with the tourist-shy locals. Hilda's also serves meals, and good seafood can be had at a handful of unpretentious places like the **Fisherman's Corner Restaurant** (757/891-2900), where you may well be served by the person who caught your meal (or his sister).

Bike rentals are available on Tangier Island, no part of which is more than five feet above sea level.

Eastville

You can get a good idea of just how rural and quiet life is on Virginia's Eastern Shore by visiting **Eastville** (pop. 281), the seat of Northampton County. A mile west of US-13 on a well-marked business loop, Eastville centers on the redbrick courthouse and old county jail, with a handful of even older buildings dating back to the mid-1700s. Eastville has an excellent roadside crab shack along US-13: the **Great Machipongo Clam Shack** (757/442-3800) has crabmeat sandwiches, fresh steamed clams, and an astonishing variety of shellfish, most of it grown, caught, or picked by the owners.

Chesapeake Bay Bridge-Tunnel

One of the more impressive engineering feats on the East Coast is the **Chesapeake Bay Bridge-Tunnel,** which opened in 1964 at the mouth of the Chesapeake Bay and was effectively doubled in 1997 by the addition of an extra set of driving lanes. Almost 18 miles long and charging a $12 toll, the structure consists of one high-level bridge, two deep tunnels, four islands, and many miles of raised causeway. Two miles from the southern end of the bridge, a fishing pier and restaurant operate on man-made Sea Gull Island.

Before the Chesapeake Bay Bridge–Tunnel was completed in 1964, ferries linking the Eastern Shore with the mainland docked at Cape Charles, west of US 13 eight miles south of Eastville. Barges still use the harbor, ferrying freight trains across the bay.

The Chesapeake Bay Bridge-Tunnel's unique design allows for ships to pass easily, and makes for a scenic drive, day or evening.

Virginia Beach

From the toll plaza at the southern end of the Chesapeake Bay Bridge, US-60 heads east along Atlantic Avenue, passing through the woodland waterfront of **First Landing State Park** before winding up at the ocean and **Virginia Beach** (pop. 437,994), the state's most populous city and its one and only beach resort. Ten-story hotels line the main drag, Atlantic Avenue, which is plastered with large signs banning cars from "cruising" the mile-long array of funfairs, surf shops, and nightclubs.

The two deepwater harbors near Norfolk at the mouth of the Chesapeake Bay, Newport News and Hampton Roads, are the headquarters of the U.S. Navy's Atlantic Fleet and together form the world's largest naval base.

Unlike many coastal towns, Virginia Beach also boasts a significant history. Virginia's first colonists landed at Virginia Beach on April 26, 1607, before settling upriver at Jamestown; the site is marked by a stone cross at Cape Henry, at the southern lip of Chesapeake Bay. Five miles south, the excellent **Virginia Aquarium** (daily; $21; 717 General Booth Blvd.; 757/385-3474) has nearly a million gallons of sharks, sting rays, barracudas, and sea turtles, plus an IMAX theater ($8–12 extra).

If you see or hear warnings about shark attacks, take them seriously. In recent years many swimmers have been badly injured or killed by sharks, even in very shallow water.

Virginia Beach

Along with the beaches and the aquarium, one of the big attractions in Virginia Beach is breakfast, thanks to the fantastic range of places up and down Atlantic Avenue, like the **Maple Tree Pancake House** (2608 Atlantic Ave.; 757/425-6796) or **Pocahontas Pancakes** (3420 Atlantic Ave. at 35th St.; 757/428-6352).

But perhaps the best reason to stop at Virginia Beach is that accommodations are so much cheaper here than out on the Outer Banks: Dorm beds at **Angie's HI Hostel** (302 24th St.; 757/491-1830) cost around $20 a night, and the same owners offer reasonably priced rooms at the adjacent **Ocean Cove Motel** ($80 and up; 300 24th St.; 757/491-1830). Other locally run places include the **Golden Sands Inn** ($50–150; 1312 Atlantic Ave.; 757/428-1770), and campers will appreciate the fine facilities, including beaches, coastal wetlands, hiking trails, and kayaking routes, at the nearly 3,000-acre **First Landing State Park** (757/412-2300).

Virginia Beach is home to the **Association for Research and Enlightenment** (800/333-4499 or 757/428-3588, 215 67th St.), which is dedicated to continuing the legacy of early American psychic Edgar Cayce, offering classes in ESP—but you already knew that, didn't you?

Norfolk

During colonial times, **Norfolk** (pop. 242,803; pronounced "NAW-fik") was the largest city in Virginia and one of the busiest ports in North America. It's still very much connected with the water, which you can experience first-hand at the **Nauticus National Maritime Center** (daily in summer, closed Mon. rest of year; $13.95; 757/664-1000), where the engaging displays inside are dwarfed by the massive hulk of the battleship USS *Wisconsin* moored alongside. Away from the waterfront, Norfolk has a couple more worthwhile destinations, including the lovely **Chrysler Museum** (Wed.–Sun.; free; 245 Olney Rd.; 757/664-6200), on the north side of downtown off Duke Street. The personal art collection of Walter

DOUGLAS MacARTHUR

The **Norfolk Tides** (757/622-2222), Class AAA farm team of the Baltimore Orioles, play at beautiful Harbor Park, off I-264 at Waterside Drive, where you can watch big ships sail past. Games are broadcast on **WGH 1310 AM.**

Chrysler, the self-educated engineer who created one of the "Big Three" car companies and built New York's Chrysler Building, is displayed inside a commodious Italianate building. Norfolk, a staunch Navy town, also holds the final resting place of controversial U.S. Army general Douglas MacArthur, preserved alongside his personal papers (and his 1950 Chrysler Imperial limousine) at the **MacArthur Memorial** (Tues.–Sun.; free; 757/441-2965), inside Norfolk's old City Hall building at Bank and Plume Streets downtown.

Even if you're just racing through, bound for the beach, Norfolk has one place where you really ought to stop and eat: **Doumar's Cones and BBQ** (757/627-4163), a half mile north of downtown at 19th Street and Monticello Avenue. Besides being a real old-fashioned drive-in, this place stakes a claim to having invented the ice cream cone, since the owner's uncle, Abe Doumar, sold the first ones at the 1904 St. Louis World's Fair. Doumar's still sells great handmade cones, barbecue sandwiches, and a deliciously thirst-quenching limeade. Pass by at your peril. . . .

From Norfolk, you can take US-17 south across the aptly named Great Dismal Swamp or follow the faster Hwy-168, which takes you past a feast of roadside fruit stands, barbecue shacks, and junk shops, straight down to Kitty Hawk and the Outer Banks of North Carolina.

NORTH CAROLINA

Wild Atlantic beaches, a handful of tiny fishing villages, and some of the country's most significant historic sites make coastal North Carolina a great place to visit. A highlight for many vacationers is the **Outer Banks,** miles of barrier islands where busy resort towns like

Nags Head contrast with the stretches of pristine beaches protected on the **Cape Hatteras National Seashore.** Besides golden sands, the Outer Banks area includes two evocative historic sites: the dunes at **Kitty Hawk,** where the Wright Brothers first took to the air, and **Roanoke Island,** site of the first ill-fated English effort to colonize the New World. Farther south, beyond the quirky, small city of **Wilmington,** a movie-making mecca, the 300-mile coastal route turns inland around **Cape Fear,** heading toward the South Carolina border.

Kitty Hawk:
The Wright Brothers National Memorial

Alternately known as Killy Hauk, Kitty Hock, and Killy Honk before its current name came into general use, **Kitty Hawk** to most people means one thing: the Wright broth-

First flight: 120 feet in 12 seconds. Orville mans the plane, Wilbur runs alongside.

ers' first powered airplane flight more than a century ago, on December 17, 1903. Lured by the steady winds that blow in from the Atlantic and by the high sand dunes that cover the shore, Wilbur and Orville Wright first came to the Outer Banks in 1900 and returned every year thereafter with prototype kites and gliders built out of bicycle parts, which they fine-tuned to create the world's first airplane. Their tale is truly one of the great adventure and success stories of the modern age, and the site of their experiments has been preserved as the **Wright Brothers National Memorial.** First stop is the **visitors center** (daily; $4; 252/441-7430), which includes a number of exhibits tracing the history of human efforts to fly. Every hour, rangers give engaging talks alongside a full-sized replica of the Wright brothers' first plane.

Orville Wright   Wilbur Wright

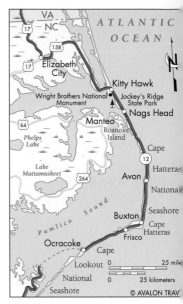

The most affecting aspect of the memorial is the unchanged site where the brothers first flew. Each of the first four flights is marked by stones set on the grassy field. The first flight, with Orville at the controls flying into a 25-mph headwind, lasted 12 seconds and covered just 120 feet—barely more than a brisk walking pace. The 90-foot-high sand dune where Wilbur and Orville first took to the air has been planted over with grasses to keep it from blowing away. Paths climb to the top of the dune, where a 60-foot, wing-shaped granite pylon is inscribed with these words:

In commemoration of the conquest of the air by the brothers Wilbur and Orville Wright. Conceived by genius, achieved by dauntless resolution and unconquerable faith.

The park is off US-158, on the inland side of the highway, two miles south of the Wright Memorial Bridge from the mainland. Though the memorial is definitely worth an extended visit, the towns around it are a bit disappointing—both Kitty Hawk and Kill Devil Hills are little more than narrow strips of commercial development.

Jockey's Ridge State Park

The windswept 110-foot-high twin sand dunes of **Jockey's Ridge State Park** (daily; free; 252/441-7132) tower over US-158 between Kitty Hawk and Nags Head. The highest sand dunes on the East Coast, Jockey's Ridge barely survived being bulldozed in the 1970s to form yet another Outer Banks resort; it's now one of the prime hang-gliding spots in the country—remember the Wright brothers! Jockey's Ridge is also a nice place to wander the short boardwalk nature trail that points out the diverse plants and animals of the dune community. You may want to take your shoes off and scamper around the sands barefoot. If you feel especially daring, **Kitty Hawk Kites** across the highway at milepost 10.5 dubs itself the "World's Largest Hang-Gliding School" and offers equipment rentals and lessons ($90 and up; 252/441-4127 or 877/359-8447), plus anything else you might need to make the most of your time here.

If you're traveling along the Carolina coast in summer, be aware that the hurricane season begins in June and lasts through the end of November. These are deadly serious storms, so take heed of any warnings, and follow the evacuation instructions broadcast over radio and TV networks.

Nags Head

The towns of the northern Outer Banks overlap each other so much it can be hard to tell you are in **Nags Head,** six miles south of Kitty Hawk. One of the oldest and most popular resorts in the region, Nags Head also offers the widest range of visitor facilities. Good places to spend a night or two include a beachfront roadside classic at milepost 16.5: the historic **Sea Foam Motel** ($75 and up; 7111 S. Virginia Dare Trail; 252/441-7320), one of the last surviving 1940s motels on the Outer Banks. The pine-paneled walls, vivid tiles, and slamming screen doors will take you back to a simpler time.

Nearby, the even more atmospheric **First Colony Inn** ($89 and up; 6715 S. Croatan Hwy.; 252/441-2343), along US-158 at milepost 16, was moved from its valuable oceanfront location to the middle of the island, but it still offers oodles of old-fashioned charm along with a delicious breakfast and afternoon tea.

The name Nags Head is derived from the practices of Outer Banks pirates, who tied lanterns around the heads of their horses to simulate boats bobbing at anchor. The lanterns lured passing ships onto shore, where they ran aground on the offshore sandbars.

One more long-standing local landmark, **Sam & Omie's** (closed in winter; 7228 S. Virginia Dare Trail; 252/441-7366), near the east end of US-64, has featured inexpensive but well-prepared family fare, three meals a day (plus a full bar), for over 70 years.

Roanoke Island:
Fort Raleigh National Historic Site

From an area known as Whalebone Junction at the south end of Nags Head, US-64 runs west over a causeway and bridge to **Roanoke Island,** site of the first English settlement in

The Outer Banks

The geography of the Outer Banks, a series of barrier islands stretching for over 200 miles along the coast of North Carolina, has changed dramatically over time, thanks to hurricanes and winter storms, not to mention human hands. Until a series of lighthouses was built beginning in the late 18th century, the islands and the offshore shoals were so treacherous they became known as the "Graveyard of the Atlantic."

Nowadays, the same places where pirates once plundered are given over to windsurfing, hang-gliding, kite-surfing, sportfishing, and beachcombing, as the Outer Banks (sometimes abbreviated OBX) have become a tourist and recreation destination par excellence. The resident population of some 33,920 swells to accommodate over six million annual visitors, but unlike its nearest comparison, Cape Cod, the Outer Banks area boasts only a few historic towns. Instead, substantial development during the 1990s building boom has covered the sands with an ugly sprawl of vacation homes and time-share condos perched—often on stilts to protect them from storm damage—directly on the broad Atlantic beaches. Most of the development has taken place in the north along two parallel roads: US-158, usually called The Bypass but also known as Croatan Highway; and oceanfront Hwy-12, a.k.a. Virginia Dare Trail and Beach Road. Mileposts on both roads mark distances from north to south. There's plentiful lodging in the many little towns along Hwy-12; gas stations and fast-food restaurants line US-158. The exception to the commercial sprawl is the magical 75 miles of the Cape Hatteras National Seashore.

Along the northern Outer Banks, bridges link Nags Head and Kitty Hawk with the mainland, though access to the less-developed southern parts of the Outer Banks is limited to ferry boats, all of which carry cars.

North America. The legendary "Lost Colony" was first established in 1584 by Sir Walter Raleigh, but the effort was not a success, and the survivors returned to England. In 1587, a larger expedition of 117 colonists arrived,

Raleigh's flagship, *Ark Raleigh*

including women and children, but because of the outbreak of war with Spain and the manifold difficulties involved in crossing the Atlantic Ocean, there was no further contact with England until 1590.

By the time the next supply ship returned, the settlers had disappeared without a trace, which prompted numerous theories about their fate. Now, amid an eerily dark forest, the colony's original earthwork fortress has been excavated and reconstructed as the centerpiece of the **Fort Raleigh National Historic Site.** Exhibits inside the **visitors center** (daily; free; 252/473-5772) include a few rusty artifacts and dry displays explaining the historical context of the colonial effort. There are also copies of the many beautiful watercolors and drawings of native plants, animals, and people produced by the original expedition's two immensely talented scientists, John White and Thomas Hariot.

Hundreds of ancient ships and unfortunate sailors met their watery end in the shallow waters off Cape Hatteras. The remains of over 2,000 vessels lie along the entire Carolina coastline; a few are visible from shore at low tide.

Throughout the summer, a waterfront theater adjacent to Fort Raleigh presents a popular production of *Lost Colony*, which dramatizes the events of the ill-fated settlement. Call for details or tickets ($20–24 adults, $10 under 12; 252/473-3414).

The historic port of **Manteo** (pop. 1,052; pronounced "MAN-tee-o"), in the middle of Roanoke Island between Fort Raleigh and the beach resorts of the Outer Banks, was named for the Native American who helped Sir Walter Raleigh and the Lost Colony. Manteo is the only county seat in North Carolina that's located on an island. You can still sense the town's proud seagoing history as you walk along the quiet streets near the tidied-up waterfront. Surrounded by pleasure boats, the main attraction here is the *Elizabeth*

II (daily Mar.–Dec.; $8), a full-sized, square-rigged replica of the type of ship that carried colonists here from England 400-odd years ago.

Cape Hatteras National Seashore

The first piece of coastline to be protected as a national park, **Cape Hatteras National Seashore** stretches for 75 miles along the Atlantic Ocean. Starting in the north at Nags Head, and continuing south along slender Bodie, Hatteras, and Ocracoke Islands, the area preserved within Cape Hatteras National Seashore is the largest undeveloped section of coastline on the East Coast, providing an increasingly rare glimpse of nature amid ever-encroaching development. The few old fishing villages that stood here when the seashore was set aside in the 1930s are unfortunately exempt from the anti-development prohibitions of the national seashore; these have grown ugly and unwieldy. Nevertheless, the many miles in between remain almost entirely untouched.

> Warmed by the Gulf Stream currents, the Outer Banks beaches are some of the best in the world, but the waters do not warm up appreciably until south of Oregon Inlet, and swimming in the northern stretches remains quite invigorating until July.

For many visitors, the highlight of the national seashore is the historic **Cape Hatteras Lighthouse,** a mile west of Hwy-12 at the south end of Hatteras Island. Others come here to enjoy the warm waters and strong, steady winds—two areas of Pamlico Sound on the inland side of Cape Hatteras have been set aside for windsurfers, dozens of whom flock here on summer days to what's considered one of the finest sailboarding and kite-surfing spots in the United States. And of course, there are miles of open beaches, perfect for aimless strolling.

At the north end of Cape Hatteras, eight miles south of Nags Head, there's a national seashore **visitors center** (daily;

Cape Hatteras Lighthouse

Hurricanes

If you're traveling along the East Coast in late summer, be aware that the farther south you go the more likely you are to encounter one of Mother Nature's most powerful phenomena, the hurricane. All across the southeastern United States, hurricane season begins in June and lasts through November, and the threat of a storm can put a sudden end to the summer fun. Hurricanes are tropical storms covering upwards of 400 square miles, with winds reaching speeds of 75 to 150 mph or more. These storms form as far away as Africa, and sophisticated warning systems are in place to give coastal visitors plenty of time to get out of harm's way. Radio and TV stations broadcast storm watches and evacuation warnings, and if you hear one, heed it and head inland to higher ground.

Even more dangerous than the high winds of a hurricane is the storm surge—a dome of ocean water that can be 20 feet high at its peak, and 50 to 100 miles wide. Ninety percent of hurricane fatalities are attributable to the high waves of a storm surge, which can wash away entire beaches and intensify flooding in coastal rivers and bays many miles upstream from the shore. The strongest hurricane recorded in the United States was the Labor Day storm of 1935, which killed 500 people and destroyed the Florida Keys Railroad. More recent hurricanes include Hurricane Irene in 2011, the multiple 'canes that pounded Florida in 2004, and Hurricane Andrew in 1992. The levee breaks that flooded New Orleans made August 2005's Hurricane Katrina by far the most costly U.S. storm, at some $85 billion, but the deadliest hurricane on record

hit Galveston Island, Texas, early in September 1900, killing more than 6,000 people—in human terms by far the worst natural disaster in United States history.

252/473-2111) and a nature trail winding along Pamlico Sound at the foot of **Bodie Island Lighthouse,** the first of three historic towers along the Hatteras coast. On the ocean side of Hwy-12, **Coquina Beach** has a broad strand, lifeguards and showers in summer, and the remains of a wooden schooner that was wrecked here in the 1920s.

The section of Pamlico Sound known as **Canadian Hole,** between the towns of Avon and Buxton, is rated as one of the best windsurfing spots on the East Coast.

Continuing south, across the Oregon Inlet (where there's a first-come, first-served campground), Hwy-12 runs through the 5,800-acre **Pea Island National Wildlife Refuge,** which was established in 1937 to protect the nesting grounds of loggerhead sea turtles, as well as the coastal wetlands essential to the survival of the greater snow goose and other migratory waterfowl. South of the refuge, a few short barrages of vacation condos and roadside sprawl—go-kart parks, mini-golf courses, and a KOA Kampground—line the highway between Rodanthe and Salvo, before the road reaches the heart of the park, where high sand dunes rise along 15 miles of undeveloped oceanfront.

Avon and Buxton: Cape Hatteras Lighthouse

At the rough midpoint of Hatteras Island, the vacation town of **Avon** stretches for a couple of miles along Hwy-12 before the road hits the Canadian Hole windsurfing area, two miles south of town. After another few miles of natural dunes,

Cape Hatteras Lighthouse, Cape Hatteras, N.C.

the road bends sharply to the west; continuing south here brings you to the main **Cape Hatteras National Seashore visitors center** (daily in summer only; 252/995-4474) and the famous **Cape Hatteras Lighthouse.** At 210 feet, the black-and-white-striped lighthouse is the tallest brick lighthouse in the United States, visible from as far as 25 miles. However, because the ocean here has been slowly eroding away the beach (when the lighthouse was built in 1870, it was a quarter mile from the waves; by 1995 the coast was a mere 120 feet away from its base), in 1999 the National

Blackbeard the Pirate

Wandering around the idyllic harbor of Ocracoke, it's hard to imagine that the waters offshore were once home to perhaps the most ferocious pirate who ever sailed the Seven Seas— Blackbeard. The archetypal pirate, even in his

Capture of the Pirate, Blackbeard, 1718

day, when piracy was common, Blackbeard was famous for his ruthlessness and violence as much as for his long black beard and exotic battle dress, wearing six pistols on twin gunbelts slung over his shoulders and slashing hapless opponents with a mighty cutlass. His pirate flag featured a heart dripping blood and a skeleton toting an hourglass in one hand and a spear in the other.

For all his near-mythic status, Blackbeard's career as a pirate was fairly short. After serving as an English privateer in the Caribbean during Queen Anne's War, in 1713 Blackbeard (whose real name was Edward Teach) turned to piracy, learning his trade under the pirate Benjamin Hornigold. Outfitted with four stolen ships, 40 cannons, and a crew of 300 men, Blackbeard embarked on a reign of terror that took him up and down the Atlantic coast of the American colonies. After five years of thieving cargoes and torturing sailors, Blackbeard was confronted off Ocracoke by forces led by Lt. Robert Maynard of the Royal Navy, and during a ferocious battle on November 22, 1718, the pirate and most of his men were killed. Blackbeard himself was stabbed 25 times, and his head was sliced off and hung like a trophy on the bowsprit of his captor's ship.

Though there is no evidence that he ever buried any treasure anywhere near Ocracoke, Blackbeard's ship, the *Queen Anne's Revenge*, was discovered in 1996 off Bogue Bank, and some cannons and other objects recovered from the pirate's ship are being preserved by the North Carolina Maritime Museum in Beaufort. Blackbeard's legend, to be sure, lives on.

The village of Frisco, five miles north of the Hatteras ferry terminal, holds the small but surprisingly good **Native American Museum** (closed Mon.; $5; 252/995-4440), which boasts an extensive collection of artifacts from several tribes, including those from the Cape Hatteras area, and Hopi and Navajo crafts.

Park Service succeeded in lifting the 3,000-ton lighthouse onto rails and shifting it a quarter mile inland. If you feel fit, climb the stairs (12 stories' worth, each way; $7) to the top of the lighthouse for a grand view—one that gives the clearest sense of just how narrow and transitive the Outer Banks really are.

Farther along, at the end of this road, there's a summer-only, first-come, first-served campground.

From the Cape Hatteras Lighthouse, Hwy-12 bends west and south through **Buxton** and **Frisco,** where you will find a gauntlet of motels, gas stations, and fast-food restaurants at the commercial center of Cape Hatteras. The very good and very popular **Fish House** (252/995-5151), on Hwy-12 next to Cape Hatteras High School, doesn't look like much from the road, but the fish here is fresh daily. Buxton's motels, like the **Lighthouse View** (252/995-5680 or 800/225-7651), which is right on the beach and also has a good-sized swimming pool, are reasonably priced (around $100 a night in summer) and clean. Ocean beaches here at the very tip of the cape are among the most spectacular anywhere; swimmers should note that because they are south-facing, they tend to pick up some of the most extreme surf—especially when hurricanes hit—which is why Buxton and Frisco are the local surfing capitals.

More restaurants and motels (including a Holiday Inn Express) await you in **Hatteras,** at the southern end of the island. From here, state-run ferries (5 AM–midnight; free) shuttle every half hour across to Ocracoke Island, another mostly unspoiled barrier island where you'll find great beaches and the pretty village of Ocracoke, at the island's southern tip.

Ocracoke

About the only Outer Banks town that hasn't lost its small-scale charm, **Ocracoke** is a great place to spend an afternoon or two, walking or cycling along unpaved back streets lined by overgrown gardens and weathered old homes. Since it's easy to reach from the mainland, via ferries from Swan Quarter and from Cedar Island, Ocracoke is a popular destination, but the tourism here is so low-key it still feels like a place you can discover for yourself.

The ferries from the mainland south of Ocracoke drop you at the heart of town. Coming in from the north on Hwy-12, you pass through a short strip of real estate agencies and restaurants like **Howard's Pub** (252/928-4441), a local institution whose rooftop, ocean-view deck is a very pleasant place to eat deep-fried local seafood and sample one or more of its 200 different beers.

From Hwy-12, a number of small back roads (including oak-lined Howard Street and another called simply Back Road, which runs past **Teach's Hole,** a shop dedicated to the pirate Blackbeard) are worth exploring—especially by bike, the best way to get around Ocracoke. Just south of the harbor, Point Road runs west to the squat, whitewashed 1823 Ocracoke Lighthouse.

Ocracoke Practicalities

Ocracoke's small and photogenic harbor is ringed by low-key, low-rise restaurants, bike rental stands, hotels, bars, and B&Bs. Many of the restaurants ringing the Ocracoke harbor morph into bars after dark. All are friendly and informal, and most have some kind of live music during the summer season, making wandering around town a prime visitor activity. Away from the harbor, the **Back Porch** (110 Back Rd.; 252/928-6401) is rated as one of the Outer Banks' best restaurants.

There are no chain hotels on Ocracoke (which may in itself be reason enough to visit!), and local places are generally down-to-earth, not fancy. The oldest lodging option is **Blackbeard's Lodge,** a rambling old motel across from the Back Porch ($80 and up; 111 Back Rd.; 252/928-3421). Another characterful place is the 100-year-old **Island Inn** ($75 and up; 252/928-4351), near the harbor.

Right across from the ferry landing, there's a very helpful **visitors center** (252/928-4531) that has complete information on Ocracoke and the rest of Cape Hatteras. Running between Ocracoke on Cape Hatteras, and two places on the North Carolina mainland (Cedar Island and Swan Quarter), the state-run ferry departs approximately every two hours (every three hours in winter) and takes just over 2.5 hours each way. The cost is about $15 per car, $30 for an RV; call 800/BY-FERRY for current schedules and further information.

From Cedar Island, it's close to an hour's drive along US-70 to the next big city, Beaufort.

Cape Lookout National Seashore

If you like the look of Cape Hatteras but want to avoid the crowds, plan a visit to the much wilder **Cape Lookout National Seashore,** another series of barrier islands, which stretch for 55 miles from Ocracoke to the south near Beaufort. It's accessible only by boat, and there are few roads or services once you're there, but it's a lovely place to hike or camp, collect seashells, or just wander along the peaceful shore, exploring the remains of cabins and abandoned villages. Day trips to Point Lookout leave from Beaufort on the "World's Largest Speedboat," the Lookout Express ($15; 252/728-6997), or you can usually arrange a charter from Ocracoke.

Beaufort and Morehead City

Known as Fishtown until it was renamed in 1722, the charming 18th-century town of **Beaufort** (pop. 4,189) has quiet streets lined with churches, cemeteries filled with weather-stained monuments, and whitewashed houses with narrow porches. The nautical-themed shops and restaurants along the water on busy Front Street, three blocks south of US-70, attract tourists and boaters traveling along the Intracoastal Waterway. The spacious **North Carolina Maritime Museum** (daily; free; 315 Front St.; 252/728-7317) features many informative exhibits on the region's nautical and

Not surprisingly, Beaufort, North Carolina is often confused with Beaufort, South Carolina. The former is pronounced "BO-fort"; the latter is pronounced "BYOO-furd."

natural history, as well as a truly impressive display of over 1,000 beautiful seashells. The museum also sponsors an annual **Wooden Boat Show,** held the last weekend in September.

If you're looking for a meal in Beaufort, try **Clawson's** (425 Front St.; 252/728-2133), a burger and seafood place housed in an old grocery store that's been in business since 1905.

While Beaufort may be prettier, you'll find the best food in burly **Morehead City,** three miles west of Beaufort and across the bridge. Try the homemade seafood-cocktail sauce and Tarheel hush puppies at the **Sanitary Fish Market & Restaurant** (501 Evans St.; 252/247-3111); it's easy to find amidst the sportfishing boats a block off US-70. For even more famous burgers (and shrimp burgers, and onion rings, and milk shakes, and more!), head along to **El's Drive-In** (252/726-3002), open since 1959 on US-70, three miles south of Morehead City, a mile south of the bridge to Atlantic Beach.

Bogue Bank: Fort Macon

More barrier island beach resorts line **Bogue Bank,** which runs south of Morehead City in a nearly east–west orientation for some 25 miles. The half dozen family-oriented resort towns have freely accessible—but quite often crowded—beaches. The largest, **Atlantic Beach,** across a bridge from Morehead City, has a boardwalk backed by a go-kart track and a small amusement arcade. The very enjoyable **State Aquarium** (daily; $8), five miles west of town on Hwy-58, features extensive displays on the local loggerhead sea turtles.

At the northeast end of Bogue Bank stands **Fort Macon State Park** (daily; free), which centers on a massive pre–Civil War fortress overlooking the harbor entrance. The pentagon-shaped masonry fort, completed in 1834, was captured early in the Civil War by the Confederacy. In April 1862, Union forces retook Fort Mason after a bombardment and controlled Beaufort for the rest of the war.

Camp Lejeune and Jacksonville

Midway between Beaufort and Wilmington, much of the coastline is taken over by the 100,000-acre U.S. Marine Corps base of **Camp Lejeune.** Established during World War II and now home to the crack rapid deployment forces and an urban combat training center, Camp Lejeune is open by appointment to groups interested in a nose-to-nose encounter with tanks, humvees, and other lethal machines. (Visting

North Carolina's beaches are prime nesting grounds for endangered loggerhead sea turtles. These huge turtles come ashore mid-May to late August by the light of the full moon. Females lay and bury as many as 100 eggs, then in September–October the tiny hatchlings scramble back into the sea.

groups should consist of 10–45 people, and must be recognized civic, private, or military organizations.) Sentries will check you in and out at both ends of the surprisingly scenic 25-mile drive across the base along Hwy-172, which serves as a shortcut to looping US-17.

At the northwest corner of Camp Lejeune, **Jacksonville** (pop. 80,542) is little more than a civilian adjunct to the base, with all the gas stations, fast-food franchises, and tattoo parlors Lejeune's 45,000 Marines and their dependents could want. One sobering sight is on the edge of town, just off Hwy-24 (opposite a Sonic Drive-In): the 50-foot-long granite wall of the **Beirut Memorial** remembers the more than 250 Camp Lejeune Marines killed in Beirut in 1983 by a suicide bomber. Alongside a list of their names are the words "They Came in Peace."

Wrightsville Beach

South of Camp Lejeune, US-17 runs through the lushly forested lowlands around Holly Ridge, while Hwy-210 cuts across a series of narrow barrier islands. The waterfront is mostly private, backed by beach house after beach house (rentals aplenty, if you can manage to stay for a full week), but with a few parking areas for passing travelers. The clean strands and clear blue waters continue through sleepy Topsail Beach, home to a homespun hospital for injured loggerhead turtles, the **Karen Beasley Sea Turtle Rescue & Rehabilitation Center** (822 Carolina Blvd.). The 20-odd "patients" are cared for by volunteers at the center downtown, across from the water tower.

Most of this stretch of coastline is dedicated to low-key, by-the-week family vacations, but the town of **Wrightsville Beach** has a bit more going on.

sunrise on Wrightsville Beach, seen from Blockade Runner Resort

Located 10 miles east of US-17 via US-74 or US-76, it's not all that different from dozens of other coastal vacation communities, but proximity to the lively city of Wilmington makes it a great place to stop. Places

U.S.S. *North Carolina*

to stay along the beach include the comfortable **Blockade Runner Resort** ($99–300; 275 Waynick Blvd.; 910/256-2251), which has a good restaurant, two bars, and bicycle, boat, and kayak rentals.

Wilmington

Though it's surrounded by the usual miles of highway sprawl, the downtown business district of **Wilmington** (pop. 106,476) is unusually attractive and well preserved, its many blocks of historic buildings stepping up from the Cape Fear River waterfront. The largest city on the North Carolina coast, Wilmington was of vital importance to the Confederate cause during the Civil War, when it was the only southern port able to continue exporting income-earning cotton, mostly to England, in the face of the Union blockade. Wilmington also played an important role before and during the Revolution, first as a center of colonial resistance, and later as headquarters for British general Cornwallis.

Despite its lengthy and involved military history, Wilmington itself has survived relatively unscathed and now possesses one of the country's more engaging small-town streetscapes. Cobblestone wharves and brick warehouses line the Cape Fear River, which also provides moorage for the massive 35,000-ton battleship USS *North Carolina* (daily; $12), across the river. A couple of the warehouses, like the Cotton Exchange at the north end, have been converted to house

In the book and movie *Gone With the Wind,* dashing southern hero Rhett Butler spent the Civil War as a Wilmington-based blockade runner, evading the U.S. Navy.

Transcontinental I-40 starts in Wilmington and runs west to Southern California. The first stretch is named in honor of local basketball superstar Michael Jordan, and another sign gives the mileage to the road's western destination: Barstow, Calif. 2,554.

boutiques and restaurants. A block inland, Front Street is the lively heart of town, a franchise-free stretch of book and music stores, cafés, and other businesses that's often used by film crews attempting to re-create a typically American "Main Street" scene. Films like *Blue Velvet* and TV's teenage soap opera *Dawson's Creek* were shot at Wilmington's massive Screen Gems studio and in surrounding locales.

Thanks in large part to its significant TV and movie-making business, Wilmington has a number of excellent places to eat, like the comfortable **Caffé Phoenix** (35 N. Front St.; 910/343-1395), an excellent Italian bistro serving fresh pasta dishes and pizzas. Within stumbling distance are bars like the rough-hewn **Barbary Coast** (116 S. Front St.; 910/762-8996). For a taste of top-quality traditional Southern food—grits with everything—try the **Dixie Grill** (116 Market St.; 910/762-7280), where you can work off the calories with a game of pool.

Rates at Wilmington's many chain motels and hotels are comparatively low; try the riverfront **Hilton** ($99 and up; 301 N. Water St.; 910/763-5900).

South of Wilmington, US-17 runs inland, so if you want to stick close to the coast, take Hwy-179, which curves along the shore past the rambling towns of **Ocean Isle Beach** and **Sunset Beach** before rejoining US-17 at the South Carolina border.

Cape Fear

Though it has lent its name to two of the most terrifying movies ever made, **Cape Fear** is not at all a scary place—so long as you stay on land. The name was given to it by sailors who feared its shipwrecking shoals, and hundreds of vessels have indeed been wrecked off the cape, including dozens of Confederate blockade-runners sunk during the Civil War embargo of Wilmington harbor.

Between the east and west banks of the Cape Fear River, a ferry (800/BY-FERRY, www.ncdot.org/ferry) runs about once an hour between Fort Fisher and Southport.

South of Wilmington, US-421 runs along the east bank of the Cape Fear River through typical barrier island beach resort towns like Carolina Beach and Kure Beach. Near the south end of the island, **Fort Fisher State Historic Site** features the earthwork fortification that enabled Wilmington harbor to remain open to ships throughout most of the Civil War. The fortress looks more like a series of primitive mounds than an elaborate military installation, but its simple sand piles proved more durable against Union artillery than the heavy masonry of Fort Sumter and other traditional fortresses. A **visitors center** (daily; free; 910/458-5538) describes the fort's role, with details of the war's heaviest sea battle,

when Union ships bombarded Fort Fisher in January 1865. Surrounding lands have been left wild, and a nice outpost of the State Aquarium has tanks of local sealife.

On the west bank of the Cape Fear River, Hwy-133 winds up at the pleasure-craft harbor of **Southport,** which is the halfway point between New York City and Miami, attracting sailors traveling the Intracoastal Waterway. It's also the site of the large Brunswick nuclear power plant.

Cape Fear itself is formed by **Bald Head Island,** at the mouth of the Cape Fear River, reachable only by boat from Southport. The **Old Baldy Lighthouse** on the island is the state's oldest, built in 1817.

SOUTH CAROLINA

Just beyond the border into South Carolina, you suddenly hit the exuberant mega-tourism of the "Grand Strand," a 25-mile-long conglomeration of resort hotels, amusement arcades, and Coney Island–style Americana that centers on **Myrtle Beach,** the state's number-one tourist destination. South of here things quiet down considerably, as coastal US-17 winds past the lush lowland marshes, passing through historic **Georgetown** and numerous preserved plantations before reaching **Charleston,** one of the most gracious and engaging cities in the southern United States.

South of the Border

If the Grand Strand and Myrtle Beach haven't satisfied your need for roadside kitsch, or if you're bombing along I-95 looking for a place to take a break, head to South of the Border, the world's largest and most unapologetic tourist trap. Located just south of the North Carolina state line at I-95 exit 1, South of the Border is a crazy place with no real reason to exist, yet it draws many thousands of visitors every day to a 135-acre assembly of sombrero-shaped fast-food stands, giant video arcades, souvenir shops, and innumerable signs and statues of the South of the Border mascot, Pedro, including one that's nearly 100 feet tall.

Many roadside businesses suffered when a new Interstate or bypass left them high and dry, but in the case of South of the Border, the opposite is true. It started as a fireworks and hot dog stand along US-301 in the early 1950s, but when highway engineers decided to locate I-95 here, its middle-of-nowhere locale suddenly became prime highway frontage, and owner Alan Shafer (who died in 2001 at the age of 87) made playful use of its location (50 feet south of the state line) to create this pseudo-Mexican "South of the Border" village–cum–roadside rest stop. Though the complex itself is hard to miss, with its sombrero-clad concrete brontosaurus and 20-story Sombrero Tower giving a panoramic view of the Interstate, I-95 drivers from both directions get plenty of notice of their approach, thanks to the hundreds of garish billboards that line the road, saying silly things like "Chili Today, Hot Tamale," the subliminal messages all but forcing you to pull off and chow down on a taco or three and buy some mass-produced keepsake you'll throw away as soon as you get home.

South of the Border is open 24 hours every day, and, along with the myriad of tourist shlock, it also has two gas stations and a pleasant, 300-room motel ($55 and up; 843/774-2411).

is a nonprofit, 4,000-acre park on the lushly landscaped grounds of four colonial-era indigo and rice plantations. Oak trees laden with Spanish moss stand alongside palmettos, dogwoods, and azaleas, as well as hundreds of sculptures, including many done by the owner, Anna Hyatt Huntington, who developed the site in the 1930s. Alligators and otters play in the simulated swamp, and many species of birds fly around enclosed aviaries in a section of the gardens set aside as a wildlife park.

Across the highway is the 2,500-acre **Huntington Beach State Park** ($5 per car; 843/237-4440), which sits on land carved out of the Huntington estate that is leased to South Carolina. Besides a nice beach and a popular campground, it features the Moorish-style castle called Atalaya, Anna Huntington's studio.

Pawleys Island and Hobcaw Barony

South of the commercial chaos of Myrtle Beach, travelers in search of serene tranquility have long appreciated **Pawleys Island.** The rope hammocks for which the island is best known aptly symbolize this generally relaxed, weather-worn community, where a few traditional tin-roofed shacks mix with ever-increasing numbers of multimillion-dollar mock-antebellum mansions. It's mostly private, apart from the plush environs of **Litchfield Plantation** ($160 and up; 843/237-5300), a 600-acre resort on the grounds of a colonial-era plantation. The poet and novelist James Dickey, author of

Carry insect repellent and be prepared for mosquitoes, especially late in the afternoon, almost everywhere along the muggy South Carolina coast.

The carnivorous Venus flytrap, which Charles Darwin called "the most wonderful plant in the world," does not grow wild in any part of the world except the seacoast Carolinas.

One of the more unusual radio stations in the country, **WLGI 90.9 FM,** is operated by the Ba'hai faith and broadcasts a commercial-free mix of classic 1970s soul, contemporary jazz, and messages of peace, love, and understanding. To learn more, call 800/228-6483.

The original lyrics to Stephen Foster's song "The Old Folks at Home" began "Way down upon the Pee Dee River," though he quickly changed it to the more sonorous "Suwanee."

Deliverance, liked it so much he lived here for his last 25 years and is buried in the small Pawleys Island cemetery.

An even more extensive and intimate (and affordable) taste of the old-fashioned Lowcountry life is available just down the road from Pawleys Island. Spreading along the north bank of the Pee Dee River, a mile north of Georgetown on US-17, **Hobcaw Barony** is a 17,500-acre estate that was once the winter home of 1920s financier and New Deal–era statesman Bernard Baruch and his daughter, Belle. The extensive, mostly undeveloped grounds are home to two university research centers specializing in coastal ecology, and the main homes and plantation buildings have been kept in original condition, complete with one of very few surviving slave streets. Along with preserving these historic quarters and the regional history they represent, the nonprofit educational foundation that runs Hobcaw Barony offers half-day tours to school groups and individuals (Tues.–Fri.; $20; 843/546-4623). Tours start at the **visitors center and museum** (Mon.–Fri.; free) along US-17.

Georgetown

Site of a short-lived Spanish settlement in 1526, the first European outpost in North America, **Georgetown** later became the rice-growing center of colonial America. Bounded by the Sampit and Pee Dee Rivers and the narrow inlet of Winyah Bay, Georgetown is one of the state's few deepwater harbors and home to two huge steel and paper mills along

US-17, but its downtown district along Front Street is compact and comfortable, with dozens of day-to-day businesses and a few cafés and art galleries filling the many old buildings.

Three blocks south of US-17, at the east end of Front Street, there's a pleasant waterfront promenade, where the clock-towered old town market now houses the **Rice Museum** (closed Sun.; $7). Dioramas trace South Carolina's little-known history as the world's main rice and indigo producer, a past often overshadowed by the state's later tobacco and cotton trade. The rest of town holds many well-preserved colonial and antebellum houses, churches, and commercial buildings.

A couple of good places to eat in Georgetown include seafood specialties at the **River Room** (801 Front St.; 843/527-4110) and the locals' favorite **Thomas Café** (703 Front St.; 843/546-7776), next to the Rice Museum. For more information, or to pick up a self-guided-tour map of town, contact the **Georgetown County Chamber of Commerce** (531 Front St.; 843/546-8436 or 800/777-7705), on the waterfront.

Another South Carolina musical connection: Chubby Checker (of "The Twist" fame) was born inland from Georgetown in Spring Gully, near the town of Andrews.

Hampton Plantation and McClellanville

The Santee Delta region along US-17 between Georgetown and Charleston once held dozens of large and hugely profitable plantations. One of the best preserved of these is now the **Hampton Plantation State Park,** located 15 miles south of Georgetown, then two miles west of US-17. Spreading out along the northern edge of Francis Marion National Forest, the 320-acre grounds feature a white wooden Greek Revival manor house (tours Sat.–Tues. at 1, 2, and 3 PM; $4) that once welcomed George Washington. The manor house was later home to Archibald Rutledge, poet laureate of South Carolina from 1934 until his death in 1973.

the south facade of the Hampton Plantation house

South from Hampton Plantation along US-17, a small sign marks the turnoff to the quaint Lowcountry fishing village of **McClellanville** (pop. 413). A short drive past moss-draped oak trees brings you to the town dock, where some of the last portions of South Carolina's shrimp and crab catch get unloaded and shipped to market. But some of the local shellfish doesn't travel very far at all, ending up in the kitchens of **T.W. Graham & Co.,** housed in a former general store just up from the docks (closed Mon.; 810 Pinckney St.; 843/887-4342). Graham & Co. also grills burgers and bakes great pies, so plan to stop and spend some time here.

Cape Romain National Wildlife Refuge

Dense forests stretch west from the highway, while the unspoiled **Cape Romain National Wildlife Refuge** stretches south of McClellanville nearly to Charleston, forming one of the largest and most important sanctuaries for migratory birds on the East Coast. Thousands of great blue herons, pelicans, terns, and ducks join the resident population of wild turkeys, feral pigs, deer, and alligators. To get a glimpse of the diverse life protected here, visit the **Sewee Visitor Center** (daily; free; 843/928-3368), on US-17 at Awendaw. Exhibits inside explain the natural and human history of the region, and trails outside lead to a boardwalk viewing area and an enclosure that's home to native red wolves.

Directly across from the refuge entrance on US-17, you can appreciate other aspects of the area's culture at the homey **SeeWee Restaurant** (4808 N. US-17; 843/928-3609), a general store turned restaurant serving homemade specialties, including a fabulously rich she-crab soup (served with a shot of sherry on the side). The ambience is perfect—tin cans still fill the shelves, and local fishermen stop by to offer their catches—and the low prices and friendly people make it worth planning your trip around.

Fort Moultrie and Mount Pleasant

Sitting at the entrance to Charleston harbor, across from its better-known sibling, Fort Sumter, **Fort Moultrie** (daily; $3) overlooks the Atlantic with good views of passing ships and the city of Charleston. The location alone would make Moultrie well worth a visit, but most come because of its vital role in American military history. Originally built from palmetto logs during the Revolutionary War, and since rebuilt many times, the fort is a testament to the development of coastal defenses. Its well-preserved sections date from every major U.S. war between 1812 and World War II, when Fort Moultrie protected Charleston harbor from roving German U-boats. But the fort is most famous for its role in the events of April 1861, when Fort Moultrie touched off the Civil War by leading the bombardment of Fort Sumter.

Fort Moultrie is easy to reach. From Mount Pleasant, a suburban community on the north bank of the Cooper River across from Charleston, turn south from US-17 onto Hwy-703 and then follow signs along Middle Street to the fort.

Along with Fort Moultrie, **Mount Pleasant** itself is worth visiting for the many African sweetgrass basket-makers who set up shop along US-17. While the roadside is rapidly filling up with suburban tract-house "plantations," in the warmer months women sit and weave these intricate baskets at their ramshackle stands. Like so many other Lowcountry traditions, sweetgrass weaving may soon be a lost art, as younger women are increasingly reluctant to take on this low-paid work; it can take four to five hours to weave a basket that may sell for less than $60.

Fort Sumter National Monument

Commanding an island at the mouth of Charleston Harbor, **Fort Sumter National Monument** marks the site of the first military engagement of the Civil War. On April 12, 1861, a month after Abraham Lincoln's inauguration and four months after South Carolina had seceded from the United States, Confederate guns bombarded the fort until the Federal forces withdrew. The structure was badly damaged, but no one was killed and the fort was held by the Confederates for the next four years, by which time it had been almost completely flattened. Partly restored, but still a powerful symbol of the destruction wrought by the War Between the States, Fort

the USS *Yorktown*, at Patriot's Point

Charleston

The Charleston accent is famous throughout the South. The word "garden" here is characteristically pronounced "gyarden," and "car" is "kyar," while the long "a" of Charleston (usually pronounced "Chaaahrleston") is as distinctive as JFK's "HAAH-vahd."

Established in 1670 as the capital of South Carolina, **Charleston,** more than any other Deep South city, proudly maintains the aristocratic traditions established during the plantation era. Then the elite would flee the heat, humidity, and mosquitoes of their lowland fiefdoms and come here to cavort in ballrooms and theaters. Still ruled by old money, though no longer the state capital, Charleston is both pretentious and provincial; locals like to say that Charleston is the place where the Ashley and Cooper Rivers meet to form the Atlantic Ocean. Though there are clear divides between the haves and have-nots, Charleston is surprisingly cosmopolitan, accommodating a historic ethnic mix of French Huguenots, Catholic Acadians, and Afro-Caribbeans, who collectively introduced the wrought-iron balconies and brightly colored cottages that give the city much of its charm. George Gershwin's opera *Porgy and Bess,* for example, was inspired by life in Charleston's Creole ghetto, specifically Cabbage Row, now a tidy brick-paved alley off Church Street.

Having suffered through a devastating earthquake, two wars, and innumerable hurricanes, Charleston has rebuilt and restored itself many times, yet it remains one of the South's most beautiful cities. Impressive neoclassical buildings line the streets, especially in the older, upmarket sections of town south of Broad Street and along the waterfront Battery. Charleston's many small, lush gardens and parks make it ideal for aimless exploring on foot rather than by car. If you'd like a friendly, intelligent guide to show you around, contact Mr. Ed Grimball (843/762-0056).

Many of the mansions and churches are open to visitors, but it's the overall fabric of Charleston, rather than specific sites, that is most memorable. That said, the 1828 Greek Revival **Edmondston-Alston House** (daily; $10; 21 E. Battery) is definitely worth a look, as is the beautiful spire of **St. Michael's Episcopal Church** (daily; donations; 71 Broad St.), which was modeled on the London churches of Sir

Christopher Wren. A quarter mile north, at Church and Market Streets, is the open-air **City Market,** known as the "Ellis Island of Black America," since over a third of all slaves arrived in the colonies here. Once the commercial center of Charleston, the market now houses a range of souvenir shops and touristy restaurants.

Charleston's annual arts-and-opera **Spoleto Festival USA** (843/722-2764) is held over two weeks in May and June.

Practicalities

Thanks to its considerable tourist trade, Charleston supports a number of excellent eateries at all price ranges. In the center of town, great breakfasts (as well as lunch, dinner, and Sunday brunch) are available at the very popular **Hominy Grill** (207 Rutledge Ave.; 843/937-0930). Around the City Market, you'll find the very popular **Hyman's Seafood** (215 Meeting St.; 843/723-6000), which has a variety of basic but good-value fresh fish entrées for around $10; expect a wait. More sedate and expensive dinner places nearby include the stylish **SNOB** (Slightly North of Broad; 192 E. Bay St.; 843/723-3424) and **Magnolia's** (185 E. Bay St.; 843/577-7771), serving inventive takes on Charleston's traditional Lowcountry food.

Like its restaurants, Charleston's accommodation options tend toward the luxurious and expensive. Of the dozens of old-fashioned but well-appointed B&Bs (all of which charge upwards of $200 a night), the elegant **John Rutledge House** (116 Broad St.; 843/723-7999 or 800/476-9741) offers four-star comfort in a converted 1763 house. On the bay, fronting the Battery, the romantic, Queen Anne–style **Two Meeting Street Inn** (2 Meeting St.; 843/723-7322) has been welcoming guests for over 50 years. Hotels in and around the historic district are similarly expensive, though you'll find a very handy **Days Inn** ($125 and up; 155 Meeting St.; 843/722-8411) downtown.

Outside the historic area a half mile south of US-17, the **Charleston Visitor Center** (daily; 375 Meeting St.; 843/724-7174) is a good first stop. It is free to ride the DASH shuttle buses that follow several routes downtown.

Edmondston-Alston House

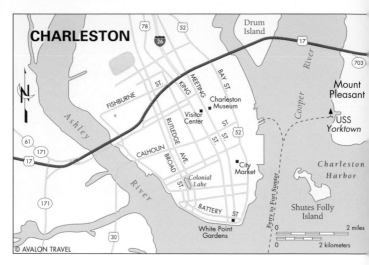

As recently as 1960, the population of South Carolina's Sea Islands was predominantly African American—10 to 1 on average. Now, with all the recent "plantation-style" vacation resorts, the proportions have effectively been reversed. As a last defense against the dark arts of resort developers, traditional African American Gullah culture is celebrated in summer festivals and tourism literature promoting the Gullah-Geechee Heritage Coast.

Sumter is a key stop on any tour of Civil War sites.

You can visit Fort Sumter by taking your personal boat or by taking a ferry tour boat ($17; 843/722-2628); they leave from the north side of Charleston Bay at Patriot's Point, just off US-17 at the foot of the soaring new cable-stayed bridge across the Cooper River. (Other boats to Fort Sumter dock at the South Carolina Aquarium in downtown Charleston.) Patriot's Point is also the anchorage of the aircraft carrier USS *Yorktown* (daily; $18), centerpiece of an excellent floating maritime museum that also includes World War II–era fighter planes, a destroyer that took part in D-Day, a Coast Guard cutter, and a Cold War–era submarine.

Beaufort

The second-oldest town in South Carolina, **Beaufort** (pop. 12,361; pronounced "BYOO-furd") is a well-preserved antebellum town stretching along a fine natural harbor. Established in 1710, Beaufort stands on the largest of some

75 islands near the Georgia border; the town is perhaps best known as the home of the massive U.S. Marine Corps Recruit Depot at nearby Parris Island, where new Marines undergo their basic training. Dozens of colonial-era and antebellum homes line Beaufort's quiet Bay Street waterfront, but only two, the **Verdier House** and the Greek Revival **Elliott House,** a block apart on Bay Street, are open to visitors. Verdier House offers tours, while the Elliott House is open as an art gallery.

Beaufort is a very enjoyable place to wander around and explore, and it has at least one great place to eat: **Blackstone's Cafe** (205 Scott St.; 843/524-4330), off the main street, where fans of the shrimp and grits and corned beef hash include local writer Pat Conroy. Places to stay include the waterfront **Best Western Sea Island Inn** (1015 Bay St.; 843/522-2090 or 800/528-1234) and the state's only four-star B&B, the lovely **Rhett House** ($160 and up; 1009 Craven St.; 843/524-9030), where the film of Conroy's *The Prince of Tides* was shot on location.

South to Savannah: Hilton Head Island

From Beaufort, the easiest way south is to follow Hwy-170 all the way to Savannah or to detour east onto I-95. Otherwise, a pleasant but potentially confusing series of two-lane roads run around Hilton Head Island across the lowlands toward Georgia.

Near the southern tip of South Carolina, **Hilton Head Island** is the largest ocean island between Florida and New Jersey. It was first settled in 1663, but only since the late 1950s, when a bridge to the mainland was completed, has it really been on the map. The deluxe, 500-room, 5,000-acre **Sea Pines Resort** ($250 and up; 32 Greenwood Dr.; 866/561-8802) is an international destination, and upscale golf courses and plantation-style estates abound around the island's 30,000 acres, as do minimalls and all the trappings of suburban America. There's also a very popular, family-friendly **Disney resort** ($175 and up; 22 Harbourside Ln.; 843/341-4100).

The "success" of Hilton Head has caused developers to set their sights on the rest of the Lowcountry, as shown by the opening of the super-plush **Palmetto Bluff** resort ($500

Along the Savannah River, which marks the boundary between South Carolina and Georgia, Eli Whitney invented the cotton gin in 1793 at Mulberry Grove plantation.

and up; 843/706-6500) at nearby Bluffton, where each of 50 waterfront cottages is outfitted with plasma TVs and a Sub-Zero fridge for that quintessential Lowcountry experience.

GEORGIA

The marshes and barrier islands that line the Atlantic
Ocean along the Georgia coast
are among the lesser-known
treasures of the eastern United
States. Geographically, the coastline consists of mostly roadless and largely unconnected islands, which makes coastal driving nearly impossible; the nearest north–south routes, I-95 and the older US-17, run roughly 15 miles inland, and only a few roads head east to the Atlantic shore. The lack of access has kept development to a minimum and has also been a boon to wildlife—well over half the coastline is protected within state and federal parks, preserves, and refuges.

The "you-can't-get-there-from-here" aspect can make it more than a little frustrating for casual visitors, but if you have the time and inclination, it also makes the Georgia coast a wonderful place to explore. One of the main car-friendly destinations along the Georgia coast is **Tybee Island** in the north, east of Savannah. Farther south, take time to explore the beautiful and history-rich **Golden Isles,** east of Brunswick. Both are great places to visit, and they offer an appetizing taste of the 100 miles of isolated shoreline Georgia otherwise keeps to itself.

Midway: The Smallest Church in America

The section of US-17 south of the Ogeechee River, off I-95 between exits 14 and 12, offers shunpikers (those who shun turnpikes; see www.shunpikers.com) a 24-mile taste of old-

style Lowland Georgia. Sometimes called the Old Atlantic Highway, it is a textbook example of how traveling the two-lane highways is superior in almost every way to hustling down the Interstates. Midway along, the coincidentally

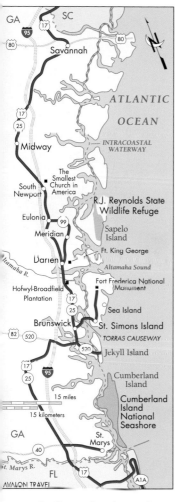

named town of **Midway** (pop. 1,500) was founded back in 1754 by a band of New England colonists, two of whom (Lyman Hall and Button Guinett) went on to sign the Declaration of Independence as Georgia's self-declared representatives to the Continental Congress. The centerpiece of Midway, then and now, is 200-year-old **Midway Church,** which preserves the original pulpit and slave gallery; keys for the church are available at the adjacent **Midway Museum** (closed Mon. and Sun.; $3; 912/884-5837).

South of Midway along US-17, a small sign on the east side of the highway (a mile south of I-95 exit 67) points travelers toward the "Smallest Church in America," a 12-seat cabin that's open 24 hours. (Please turn the lights out when you leave.) Besides the kitsch value, there's another good reason to keep an eye out for the Smallest Church: six miles east of the church, a mile from the shore down Harris Neck Road, the wonderfully named, nearly world-famous **Old School Diner** (closed Mon.–Tues.; cash only; 912/832-2136) serves up generous portions of fantastically flavorful seafood, barbecue ribs, chicken, and more. Only a half hour from Savannah, it's worth a trip from just about anywhere.

Sapelo Island and Darien

Though coastal Georgia has by and large been spared the worst excesses of real estate development, for an unforgettable taste

Savannah

Named the "Most Beautiful City in North America" by the Parisian newspaper and style arbiter *Le Monde*, **Savannah** (pop. 136,286) is a real jewel of a place. Founded in 1733 as the first settlement in Georgia, the 13th and final American colony, Savannah today preserves its original neoclassical, colonial, and antebellum self in a welcoming, un-selfconscious way. Famous for having been spared by General Sherman on his destructive March to the Sea at the end of the Civil War, it was here that Sherman made his offering of "40 acres and a mule" to all freed slaves.

Bonaventure Cemetery

Before and after the war, Savannah was Georgia's main port, rivaling Charleston, South Carolina, for the enormously lucrative cotton trade, but as commercial shipping tailed off, the harbor became increasingly recreational—the yachting competitions of the 1996 Olympics were held offshore. Savannah, home of writer Flannery O'Connor and songsmith Johnny Mercer, also served as backdrop to the best-selling book *Midnight in the Garden of Good and Evil* and numerous movies, most famously *Forrest Gump,* but it has resisted urges to turn itself into an "Old South" theme park; you'll have to search hard to find souvenir shops or overpriced knick-knack galleries.

At the center of Savannah, midway down Bull Street between the waterfront and spacious Forsyth Park, **Chippewa Square** was the site of Forrest Gump's bus bench (the movie prop was moved to the visitors center and may one day be erected in bronze). **Reynolds Square,** near the waterfront, has a statue of John Wesley, who lived in Savannah in 1736–1737 and established the world's first Sunday School here. **Wright Square** holds a monument to Chief Tomochichi, the Native American tribal leader who allowed Georgia founder James Edward Oglethorpe to settle here, and **Forsyth Park,** at the south edge of the historic center, is modeled after the Place de la Concorde in Paris, surrounded by richly scented magnolias.

Another great place to wander is **Factor's Walk,** a promontory along the Savannah River named for the "factors" who controlled Savannah's cotton trade. This area holds the Cotton Exchange and other historic buildings, many of them constructed from 18th-century ballast stones. Linked from the top of the bluffs by a network of steep stone stairways and cast-iron walkways, **River Street** is lined by restaurants, and at the east end there's a statue of a girl waving; it was erected in memory of Florence Martus, who for 50 years around the turn of the 20th century greeted every ship entering Savannah harbor in the vain hope that her boyfriend would be on board.

March is when things get crazy here in Savannah: Thousands of visitors come to the bars along Congress Street for what has grown into the world's second-largest **St. Patrick's Day** celebration—only New York City's is bigger.

One of Savannah's more unusual tourist attractions is the **Juliet Gordon Low Birthplace** (142 Bull St.), a circa-1820 house that was the childhood home of the woman who introduced Girl Scouts to America in 1912. Current Girl Scouts gain a merit badge just by walking in the door.

Practicalities

Getting around is blissfully easy: Savannah is the country's preeminent walkers' town, with a wealth of historic architecture and a checkerboard of 22 small squares shaded with centuries-old live oak trees draped with tendrils of Spanish moss, all packed together in a single square mile. Savannah's sensible and very attractive modified grid plan makes finding your way so simple that it's almost fun to try to get lost.

St. Patrick's Day celebrators

(continued next page)

(continued)

For an unforgettable midday meal, be sure to stop at **Mrs. Wilkes' Dining Room** (Mon.–Fri. 11 AM–2 PM; 107 W. Jones St.; 912/232-5997), a central Savannah home and former boardinghouse that still offers up traditional family-style Southern cooking—varying from fried chicken to crab stews, with side dishes like okra gumbo; sweet potato pie; red, green, or brown rice; and cornbread muffins. It's worth a trip from anywhere in the state—don't leave Savannah without eating here. For a more upscale take on these Deep South classics, make plans to have lunch or dinner at **The Olde Pink House**, on Reynolds Square (23 Abercorn St.; 912/232-4286). Near the Sand Gnats baseball stadium on the south side of town, right on old US-80, **Johnny Harris** (1651 E. Victory Dr.; 912/354-7810) is Savannah's oldest restaurant and one of the fanciest fried chicken and barbecue places in the world.

Road-food fans may want to head a half mile south of downtown to the **Streamliner Diner** (102 W. Henry St.), a gorgeously restored 1938 Worcester diner operated by (and across the street from) the Savannah College of Art & Design (SCAD), which has taken over many of the city's older buildings and converted them into art studios, galleries, and cafés.

Places to stay in Savannah vary from quaint B&B inns to stale high-rise hotels. For the total Savannah experience, try the **Bed and Breakfast Inn** ($150 and up; 117 W. Gordon St.; 912/238-0518), which has very nice rooms in an 1853 townhouse off Monterey Square. At the **River Street Inn** ($150 and up; 124 E. Bay St.; 912/234-6400 or 800/253-4229), well-appointed rooms fill a converted antebellum cotton warehouse, right on Factor's Walk at the heart of the Savannah riverfront. Nearby, the large **Inn at Ellis Square** ($125 and up; 201 W. Bay St.; 912/236-4440 or 800/325-2525) has good-sized hotel rooms (in a former Days Inn), right across from Factor's Walk.

The **Savannah Visitors Center** (301 Martin Luther King Blvd.; 912/944-0455), in the old Georgia Central railroad terminal just west of the historic center, has free maps and brochures and other information on the city.

of the *real* pre–tourist industry Georgia culture, make your way east to **Sapelo Island,** which stretches offshore between Midway and Darien. The island is a stark, sparsely populated, mostly undeveloped, and generally fascinating place to spend some time, a truly wild landscape where alligators and ferocious feral pigs live free among remnants of colonial-era plantation agriculture and native Creek Indian shell middens dating back 6,000 years. Once a cotton plantation, worked by slaves whose 70-odd descendants live in Hog Hammock, Sapelo's only permanent community, the island is now owned by the state of Georgia and used as a marine biology research center.

There is no real commercial development on Sapelo Island—no stores and no restaurants, so bring your own food and drink—just miles of beaches, marshlands, and open sea. Get there from the mainland hamlet of **Meridian,** where you can catch the state-run ferry for a four-hour guided tour (reservations required; adults $10, under 18 $6; 912/437-3224), which gives a full introduction to Sapelo Island life. For an even more memorable experience, arrange to stay overnight at **The Wallow** (912/485-2206), a small Hog Hammock B&B run by lifelong Sapelo Island resident Cornelia Bailey. There's a communal kitchen, or meals can be arranged in advance.

South of Sapelo Island near the mouth of the Altamaha River, which formed the rough and frequently fought-over boundary between British and Spanish parts of the New World, **Darien** (pop. 1,800) looks a lot like most other coastal Deep South towns, but it boasts a history to match many bigger or more famous destinations. After a small, 16th-century Spanish mission near here was destroyed by Native Americans, Darien was founded in 1736 by Scottish colonists (many named McIntosh, now the name of the surrounding county) near Fort King George, the first British outpost in what became Georgia. Darien later

The Class A **Savannah Sand Gnats** (912/351-9150), a Washington Nationals farm club, play at WPA-built Grayson Stadium, off US-80 on the south side of town.

A compelling nonfiction account of 1970s Darien, Melissa Fay Greene's *Praying for Sheetrock* describes how locals and legal activists used federal lawsuits to overcome the corrupt regimes of local government and law enforcement officials.

became a center of the lucrative early-19th-century rice trade, surrounded by plantations where the abuse of slaves inspired British actress Fanny Kemble's book-length indictment, *Journal of a Residence on a Georgia Plantation in 1838–39,* an influential abolitionist text.

Despite the many claims it could make to importance, Darien preserves its past in a matter-of-fact manner. The main attraction is the reconstructed **Fort King George,** a state historic site, a mile east of US-17 on Fort King George Drive (closed Mon.; $6).

Another intriguing place to visit is the **Hofwyl-Broadfield Plantation** (Thurs.–Sat.; $6), five miles south of Darien along US-17, where a well-preserved plantation home is surrounded by 1,200 acres of one-time rice fields that have reverted to cypress swamps. Displays inside the visitors center tell the story of how slaves were forced to labor in the sweltering, mosquito-plagued summer heat, building levees and doing the back-breaking work of planting, growing, and harvesting the rice.

Brunswick: The Golden Isles

Along the southeast Georgia coast, a patchwork of islands known as the **Golden Isles** offer a wide range of images and experiences. The largest and best known, **St. Simon's Island,** is a mini Hilton Head, with many vacation resorts and a sizable year-round community. The center of activity on St. Simon's is at the south tip of the island, where the village consists of a central plaza and a few blocks of shops, saloons, and restaurants along Mallery Street, which leads down to the waterfront pier and a circa-1872 lighthouse.

Georgia's most famous 19th-century poet, Sidney Lanier, settled near Brunswick after contracting tuberculosis as a POW during the Civil War. He wrote his most famous poems, including "The Marshes of Glynn," while he sat under an oak tree that stands along US-17, a mile north of town.

Sea kayaks, bicycles, and boats can be rented here, and there are a number of reasonable motels. For a carb-loading breakfast or lunch, or a taste of the Food Network's favorite Five Cheese Grilled Cheese, make your way to the popular **4th of May Café** (321 Mallery; 912/638-5444) just off Ocean Boulevard.

Also on St. Simon's, right at the heart of the island, purist wood-smoke barbecue fans flock to **Southern Soul BBQ** (2020 DeMere Rd.; 912/638-SOUL) for juicy,

St. Simon's Island Light Station

melt-in-the-mouth ribs, pulled pork sandwiches, and an excellent version of Brunswick Stew (pork, chicken, beef, corn, beans, and more mixed up in a rich tomato barbecue sauce).

Apart from the excellent food, the one real "sight" on St. Simon's Island is the **Fort Frederica National Monument,** at the northwest edge of the island, which protects the remains of the village surrounding what was once the largest fortress in the British colonies. Built in 1736 and abandoned in 1763, Fort Frederica played a vital role in keeping Georgia British, rather than Spanish; in 1742, a key battle was fought six miles south of the fort, at a site known as "Bloody Marsh."

For the total Golden Isles experience, splurge on a night or two at one of the country's plushest resorts, the five-star **Cloister Hotel** ($400 and up; 912/638-3611 or 888/SEA ISLAND), east of Fort Frederica, which covers adjacent Sea Island with 36 holes of golf courses and 264 Spanish-style rooms. Presidents from Coolidge to Bush have vacationed here, the late JFK Jr. got married here, and the G8 economic summit has been held here, too, which should give you some idea of the elite character of the place.

Back on the mainland, heavily industrialized **Brunswick** (pop. 16,500) feels about as far from the genteel pleasures of the Golden Isles as you can be. Most vacationers pass through quickly on their way to and from the Golden Isles, but there is one great place to stop: the **Georgia Pig** (912/264-6664), southwest of town at the US-17 junction, just east of I-95 exit

29. Tucked away next to a gas station in a scruffy woodland, it looks like it's been there forever; the bare-bones decor—log rafters, pine picnic tables, and creaking front door—disappears when you bite into the juicy ribs and fabulous pulled-pork sandwiches, which are smoked in a hickory-fired oven right behind the counter. Even for non-barbecue fans, Brunswick holds a road food attraction: **Willie's Wee-Nee Wagon** (3599 Altama Ave.; 912/264-1146), a yellow-and-white candy-striped diner, a mile west of US-17 across from the College of Coastal Georgia. Famous for all sorts of good things—crunchy cole-slaw, chili dogs, pork chops, steak sandwiches, and more—Willie's is something of a Georgia coast institution, and well worth searching for.

Jekyll Island

Southeast of Brunswick, and developed in the late 1880s as a private, members-only resort for New York multimillionaires, **Jekyll Island** now offers a chance for those *not* in control of a Fortune 500 company to enjoy a generous slice of Golden Isles life. Now owned by the state of Georgia, a grand hotel and dozens of palatial vacation "cottages" that would look equally at home in Newport, Rhode Island, are accessible to the general public after a long life spent catering to the richest of the rich.

At the center of the island, and the best place to start a visit, is the landmark **Jekyll Island Club Hotel** ($170 and up; 912/635-2600 or 800/535-9547). The very pleasant rooms here aren't *all* that expensive, considering the luxury you're swaddled in, and the setting is superb. Majestic oak trees dangling garlands of Spanish moss cover the 200-acre grounds, and within a short walk, many of the grand old mansions are now open for guided tours ($10). The nearby stables have been converted into a nice little **museum** (daily; free), which tells the whole Jekyll Island story.

One new development here has been the **Georgia Sea Turtle Center** ($6; 214 Stable Rd.; 912/635-4444),

Around the turn of the 20th century, the 50-odd members of the Jekyll Island Club, which included such names as Rockefeller, Carnegie, Morgan, and Vanderbilt, controlled as much as 20 percent of the world's wealth.

Georgia Sea Turtle Center, Jekyll Island

housed in the old Jekyll Island power plant. This is one of the prime places for the study and rehabilitation of these lyrical swimmers, whose native habitats have been threatened by all the housing and resort development along the Atlantic shore.

Less than a mile east, the Atlantic oceanfront is lined by Beachview Drive and a five-mile-long beach—with the least developed stretches at the north and south ends of the island. Bike rentals—which really provide the best way to see the island—are available along Beachview Drive ($5/hr; 912/635-9801).

Cumberland Island National Seashore

Right on the Florida border, and once the private reserve of the Carnegie family, the **Cumberland Island National Seashore** is a 99 percent uninhabited barrier island with miles of hiking trails and primitive backcountry camping along beaches and in palmetto forests. Also here is the unique **Greyfield Inn** (904/261-6408), the Carnegie family mansion now operated (by Carnegie heirs) as an unpretentious 16-room historic lodge that runs around $400 a night for two people, including gourmet meals and transportation from the mainland. (Bring your own bug spray!)

Unless you're a guest at the Greyfield, Cumberland Island is only accessible by a twice-daily ferry

St. Marys, Georgia, the main access to Cumberland Island, is also home to the huge Kings Bay U.S. Navy Base, home port of the nuclear-powered and -armed submarine Atlantic fleet.

($20 round-trip plus a $4 entrance fee) from the town of St. Marys, 10 miles east of I-95 exit 1. For further details, contact the Cumberland Island National Seashore information and reservations center at 912/882-4336.

FLORIDA

Stretching some 600 miles between the Georgia border and Key West at its far southern tip, Florida offers something for everyone, from unsullied nature to the tackiest tourist traps in the land, and everything imaginable in between. More than anywhere else in the United States, the Florida landscape has been designed for tourists, and no matter what your fancy or fantasy, you can live it here, under the semi-tropical sun. The many millions who visit Disney World or flock to fashionable Miami Beach each year are doing exactly what people have come to Florida to do for over a century—enjoy themselves.

Two men who made millions in the automobile industry have had immeasurable influence over the evolution of the Florida coast. Standard Oil baron Henry Flagler constructed the first railroad and built a chain of deluxe resort hotels from St. Augustine to Miami, while Carl Fisher, the developer of car headlights, promoted Florida's "Route 66," the Dixie Highway, and later helped to found Miami Beach. Their names reappear frequently wherever you travel along the Atlantic coast.

In the 1930s, when car travel and Florida tourism were both reaching an early peak of popularity, the roadside landscape was, in the words of the WPA *Guide to Florida,* lined by

. . . signs that turn like windmills; startling signs that resemble crashed airplanes; signs with glass lettering which blaze forth at night when automobile headlights strike them; flashing neon signs; signs painted with professional touch; signs crudely lettered and misspelled. They advertise hotels, tourist cabins, fishing camps, and eating places. They extol the virtues of ice creams, shoe creams, cold creams; proclaim the advantages of new cars and used cars; tell of 24-hour towing and ambulance service, Georgia pecans, Florida fruit and fruit juices, honey, soft drinks, and furniture. They urge the traveler to

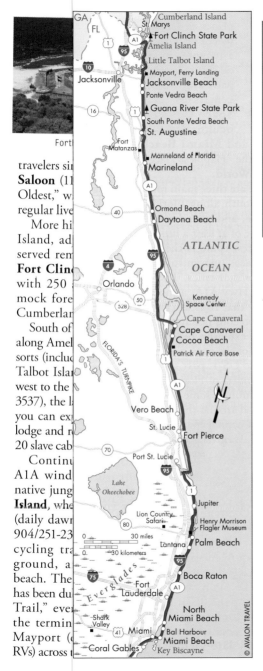

Two men who made millions in the automobile industry have had immeasurable influence over the evolution of the Florida coast. Standard Oil baron Henry Flagler constructed the first railroad and built a chain of deluxe resort hotels from St. Augustine to Miami, while Carl Fisher, the developer of car headlights, promoted Florida's "Route 66," the Dixie Highway, and later helped to found Miami Beach. Their names reappear frequently wherever you travel along the Atlantic coast.

travelers si
Saloon (11
Oldest," w
regular live
   More hi
Island, ad
served rem
Fort Clin
with 250
mock fore
Cumberlar
   South of
along Amel
sorts (inclu
Talbot Islar
west to the
3537), the l
you can ex
lodge and r
20 slave cab
   Continu
A1A wind
native jung
Island, whe
(daily dawr
904/251-23
cycling tra
ground, a
beach. The
has been du
Trail," ever
the termin
Mayport (
RVs) across

take designated tours, to visit certain cities, to stop at certain points he must see.

Despite the modern gloss of golf course estates and sprawl-ing retirement communities, which tend to overshadow the substantial stretches of wide open beaches and coastal for-est, Florida has a lengthy and fascinating history, with sig-nificant native cultures and, in **St. Augustine,** some of the oldest signs of European presence in North America, including the legendary Fountain of Youth. At the other end of the state, on the fringes of the Caribbean, **Key West** is a tropical para-dise, founded by pirates four centuries ago and still one of the most lively and anarchic places in the United States. In between, our road-trip route passes through such diverse

Of al
colonii
remair
British cri
Revolutioi
the war, the
Florida t
eventua
to the U
1821 in ex
million in i

to the sl
the very
ment, o
I-95 an
Highwa
heritage
salubrio
suggeste
tions fro
freely ar

Ameli:

Enterin
which i
Atlantic
politan
ting off
to the b
building
island i
port in
trans-Fl
Fernanc

Henry Flagler: Father of Florida Tourism

Though you've probably never heard of the man, you can't travel very far along the east coast of Florida without coming under the influence of Henry Flagler, who almost single-handedly turned what had been swampy coastline into one of the world's most popular tourist destinations. After making a fortune as John D. Rockefeller's partner in the Standard Oil Company, in the early 1880s Flagler came to St. Augustine with his wife, who was suffering from health problems. He found the climate agreeable, but the facilities sorely lacking, so he embarked on construction of the 540-room Hotel Ponce de León, which opened in 1888. The hotel, the first major resort in Florida, was an instant success, and Flagler quickly expanded his operations, building the first railroad along the coast south to Palm Beach, where he opened the world's largest hotel, the now-demolished Royal Poinciana, in 1894, joined by The Breakers in 1901 and his own palatial home, Whitehall, in 1902.

Meanwhile, Flagler was busy extending his railroad south, effectively founding the new city of Miami in 1897 when he opened the deluxe Royal Palm Hotel. From Miami, he decided to extend his Florida East Coast Railway all the way to Key West, which at the time was Florida's most populous city and the American deep-water port closest to the proposed Panama Canal. At a cost of $50 million and hundreds of lives, this amazing railroad was completed in 1912, but it lasted only two decades before a hurricane destroyed the tracks in 1935. The remnants of Flagler's railroad were used as the foundation for today's Overseas Highway, US-1, but Flagler himself never lived to see it: In 1913, a year after his railroad reached Key West, Henry Flagler fell down a flight of stairs and died at age 84.

Jacksonville Beach

East of Jacksonville, at the mouth of the St. Johns River, Hwy-A1A curves around a large U.S. Navy base (third largest in the U.S., specializing in helicopters, which you'll often see hovering overhead), past the busy Bath Iron Works shipyard and the sizable fishing port of **Mayport,** where you can enjoy a quick bite at seafood shack **Singleton's** (4728 Ocean St.; 904/246-4442) 100 yards west of the ferry landing. From Mayport, Hwy-A1A zigzags inland south and east, reaching the water again at **Jacksonville Beach,** a welcoming, family-oriented community with the usual gauntlet of cafés, mini-golf courses, and video arcades, and a nice beachfront centering on a small pier.

Class AA farm club for the Florida Marlins, the Jacksonville Suns play ball at a very nice $35 million downtown stadium called the Baseball Grounds (904/350-2040).

Host of the 2005 Super Bowl, **Jacksonville,** which covers over 840 square miles, is the largest city by area in the continental United States.

South of Jacksonville Beach spreads the enclave of **Ponte Vedra Beach,** where country club resorts replace roadside sprawl. Hwy-A1A bends inland through here, so if you want to keep close to the shore (most of which is private), follow Hwy-203 instead, rejoining Hwy-A1A on the edge of town.

South of Ponte Vedra, Hwy-A1A passes a pair of beachfront state parks (the marvelous 12,000-acre **Guana River** and smaller **South Ponte Vedra**), both of which give access to usually uncrowded sands.

Fountain of Youth

North of St. Augustine, Hwy-A1A cuts inland from the shore, crossing a bridge over the North River, then following San Marco Avenue south into the center of St. Augustine past the Fountain of Youth. That's right, the Fountain of Youth. Though its efficacy has never been proven in court, there is an actual site where Spanish explorer Ponce de León, searching for a fabled spring that would keep him forever young, came ashore in 1513. Now a pleasant 20-acre park, facing Matanzas

Bay about a mile north of central St. Augustine, the **Fountain of Youth** (daily 10 AM–4 PM; $10; 800/356-8222) preserves a naturally sulfurous spring (which you can drink from using Dixie cups—though there are no guarantees of immortality!), a burial ground, and remnants of a native Timucuan village and an early Spanish settlement.

St. Augustine

If you like history, architecture, sandy beaches, bizarre tourist attractions—or any combination of the above—you'll want to spend some time in St. Augustine. The oldest permanent settlement in the United States—though Santa Fe, New Mexico, makes a strong counterclaim to this title—**St. Augustine** was founded in 1565, half a century after Ponce de León first set foot here in 1513, looking for the Fountain

of Youth. Under Spanish control, the town's early history was pretty lively, with Sir Francis Drake leveling the place in 1586. The British, after trading Cuba for Florida at the end of the Seven Years' War, took control in 1763 and held St. Augustine throughout the American Revolution—during which Florida was staunchly loyal to King George. It served for many years as capital of Florida under both the British and Spanish, but after the Americans took over, the city lost that status to Tallahassee. St. Augustine subsequently missed out on much of Florida's 20th-century growth and development, which has allowed the preservation of its substantial historical remnants.

Across the street from the Ripley's Believe It or Not!, a coquina stone ball known as the Zero Milepost marks the eastern end of the **Old Spanish Trail,** one of the earliest transcontinental highways. Marked and promoted from here west to San Diego, the Old Spanish Trail, like the Lincoln Highway and the Dixie Highway, preceded the system of numbered highways (Route 66 et al.) and provided a popular cross-country link.

The heart of St. Augustine is contained within a walkably small area, centered on the Plaza de la Constitución, which faces east onto Matanzas Bay. Pedestrianized St. George Street runs north and south

Quaint Old St. George Street, St. Augustine, Florida

The Oldest City in the United States

from here through the heart of historic St. Augustine, while two blocks west stands the city's most prominent landmarks: two grand, early 1900s hotels—the **Ponce de Leon** and the **Alcazar.** They were orig-inally owned and operated as part of Henry Flagler's Florida empire but now respectively house **Flagler College** and the decorative arts collections of the **Lightner Museum** (daily; $10). Both are full of finely crafted interior spaces and well worth a look.

Though it's the compact size and overall historic sheen of St. Augustine that make it such a captivating place to spend some time, there are lots of individual attractions hawking themselves as important "historic sites," usually the oldest this-or-that in Florida, or even in the whole United States. The **Oldest Wooden Schoolhouse** (14 St. George St.), in the heart of historic St. Augustine, dates from 1750 and now features a push-button wax dummy of a schoolteacher, while the **Oldest Store Museum,** a block south of the main plaza (4 Artillery Ln.), has 100,000 items, all of them well past their turn-of-the-20th-century sell-by date. At the north end of St. George Street, an original city gate leads across San Marco Avenue (Hwy-A1A) to another must-see tourist trap: the original **Ripley's Believe It or Not!** museum (daily; $14.95; 904/824-1606), an elaborate Spanish Revival mansion filled since 1950 with Robert Ripley's personal collection of oddi-ties. Outside, in the parking lot, is a four-room "tree house," carved out of a California redwood tree in 1957.

These are fun in a tongue-in-cheek way, but the most im-pressive historic site is the remarkable **Castillo de San Marcos** (daily; $6), which dominates the St. Augustine waterfront. Built by Spain between 1672 and 1695, the Castillo saw its first battle in 1702, when British forces laid siege for 50 days but were unable to capture it, though they did once again level the adjacent town of St. Augustine. The Castillo was later used by the British to house American POWs during the Revolutionary War, and by the United States to house Native American pris-oners captured during the Seminole War of 1835–1842 as well as during the later Indian Wars of the Wild West. Since 1924 it's been a national monument and is open for walks along the ramparts and for frequent ranger-guided tours.

One of many attractive things about St. Augustine is the almost total lack of franchised fast-food restaurants, at least in the historic downtown area. Instead, you can choose from all sorts of local places, like the **Florida Cracker Cafe** (81 St. George St.; 904/829-0397), a casual seafood grill where you can sample the local delicacy, alligator tail. For fish-and-chips, try the **Mill Top Tavern** (19½ St. George St.; 904/829-2329), which boasts good live music and a block-long bar. (Yes, it's a short block.) Another fun place to while away an evening is **Scarlett O'Hara's,** offering beers, burgers, and live music a block from Flagler College(70 Hypolita St.; 904/824-6535). Fun and fairly good value, east of the historic core but right on lovely St. Augustine Beach itself, **Paula's Beachside Grill** (6896 Hwy-A1A; 904/471-3463) is a very popular tiki bar–style burger, sandwich, and beer stand.

Unfortunately for present-day visitors, the grand old Ponce de León Hotel no longer welcomes overnight guests, but contemporary St. Augustine does offer a wide variety of accommodations, including the imaginatively named **Beachfront B&B** ($129 and up; 1 F St.; 904/461-8727) in St. Augustine Beach, where you can spend the night in one of six tastefully decorated suites in a historic home, then wake up to watch the porpoises cavorting offshore. In the historic district, the **Kenwood Inn** ($125 and up; 38 Marine St.; 904/824-2116) has 14 rooms in a Victorian-era hotel along the Matanzas River.

For additional listings, maps, and general information, your first stop should be the **St. Augustine visitors center** (904/825-1000 or 800/653-2489), across from the Castillo.

Alligator Farm

From the heart of St. Augustine, Hwy-A1A crosses over the Matanzas River on the lovely, historic Bridge of Lions to Anastasia Island, bound for the Atlantic beaches three miles to the east. On the way to the beach, just two miles south of Old Town St. Augustine on Anastasia Boulevard (Hwy-A1A), sits one of the greatest of Florida's many tourist traps, **Alligator Farm** (daily; $21.95; 904/824-3337). Touted as the world's only complete collection of crocodilians, this was the first and is now one of the last of many such roadside menageries. A legitimate historical landmark, Alligator Farm is

Alligator Farm resident

also a fun and informative place to spend some time—great for kids and anyone who finds gators and crocs (and turtles, iguanas, monkeys, and tropical birds, all of which are here) to be captivating creatures. Start at the largest enclosure, a mossy pond seething with hundreds of baby gators (which you can feed), and be sure to pay your respects to Gomek, the Alligator Farm's massive taxidermied mascot, and to Maximo, a 16-foot Aussie crocodile who's still growing ever-larger.

Across from Alligator Farm, a road turns east from Hwy-A1A to **Anastasia State Recreation Area,** the site where the stone for Castillo de San Marcos was quarried, and where in addition to beaches there's an inlet set aside for windsurfing, hiking trails through coastal hammock forests, and a nice campground (904/461-2033) amid stately live oaks and magnolia trees.

Sulawesi Red-knobbed Hornbills at Alligator Farm

Marineland

Eighteen miles south of St. Augustine, 35 miles north of Daytona Beach, the original sea-creature amusement park, **Marineland** (daily; $8.50; 904/471-1111), opened with a

About three miles north of Marineland, on the inland side of Hwy-A1A, you can see the 16-foot-thick stone walls of **Fort Matanzas,** built by the Spanish around 1736 and never conquered. Now a national historic site, it's open for free tours.

"splash" in 1938 and closed down suddenly in 1998, declaring bankruptcy after struggling for years to compete with the much-larger likes of Sea World and Disney World. Marineland, which is credited with the first performing dolphins (and with playing a key role in the sci-fi movie *Creature from the Black Lagoon*), reopened in 2005 on a much smaller scale, with an "edutainment" focus on offering intimate encounters with its famous dolphins. It sounds like a magical experience, but before you mention Marineland to your kids, be warned: these "Swim with a Dolphin" programs cost around $200 per person—and up.

Continuing along the coast south of Marineland, you start to see roadside fruit stands advertising "Indian River Fruit"—something you'll see more of as you travel south. This is a major citrus-growing region. This stretch of Hwy-A1A, around the town of Flagler Beach, is also one of the few where you can actually see the ocean from the road.

Daytona Beach

Offering a heady barrage of blue-collar beach culture, **Daytona Beach** (pop. 68,128) is a classic road-trip destination in every way, shape, and form. The beach here is huge—over 20 miles long, and 500 feet wide at low tide—and there's

a small and recently pretty scruffy amusement pier at the foot of Main Street. The rest of Daytona Beach is rather rough at the edges, with boarded-up shops and some lively bars and nightclubs filling the few blocks between the beach area and the Halifax River, which separates the beach from the rest of the town.

The winning car of each year's Daytona 5 remains on display in the Daytona 500 Experience until the following year's rac

Besides being a living museum of pop culture, Daytona Beach has long played an important role in car culture: In the first decades of the 20th century, a real Who's Who of international automotive pioneers—Henry Ford, R. E. Olds, Malford

Duesenberg, and more—came here to test the upper limits of automotive performance. The first world land-speed record (a whopping 68 mph!) was set here in 1903, and by 1935 the ill-starred British racer Malcolm Campbell had raised it to 276 mph.

The speed racers later moved west to Bonneville Salt Flats in Utah, and Daytona became the breeding ground for stock car racing—today's Daytona 500 started out as a series of 100- to 200-mile races around a rough four-mile oval, half on the sands and half on a paved frontage road. The circuit races, both for cars and motorcycles, really came into their own after World War II. In 1947, NASCAR (the National Association for Stock Car Auto Racing) was founded here as the nascent sport's governing body, but the races soon outgrew the sands, and in 1958 they were moved to the purpose-built **Daytona International Speedway,** on US-92 six miles west of the beach, right off I-95 exit 87. Daytona offers "ride-alongs" and on-track driving experiences (for a mere $150 to $2,500). After a visit, you may want to spend some time practicing your skills at the **Speed Park** go-kart and drag racing track across the street (201 Fentress Blvd.; 386/253-3278).

Adding to Daytona's already broad mix of pop culture icons is the **Hamburger Hall of Fame** (tours by appointment; 386/254-8753). This wacky collection of burger-related memorabilia is displayed in the private home of burgermeister Harry Sperl.

Daytona Beach is party central during March and April, when some 300,000 college kids escape from northern climes to defrost and unwind with a vengeance. There has been a concerted effort to keep a lid on things recently, but if you're after peace and quiet you should head somewhere else. The same is true of the springtime **Bike Week** before the Daytona 200 in March, and again in fall during **Biketoberfest,** when thousands of motorcycling enthusiasts descend upon Daytona for a week or more of partying in between races at Daytona Speedway. The granddaddy of all stock car races, the

The town of **Ormond Beach,** which adjoins the north side of Daytona Beach, was also used by early speed-seekers. Prior to that, it was a winter playground of the rich and famous, richest and most famously John D. Rockefeller, who wintered here for years before his death in 1937 at age 97. His mansion, called **The Casements,** is now a museum (25 Riverside Dr.; 386/676-3216) along the east bank of the Halifax River.

Daytona 500, is held around Valentine's Day, but getting one of the 110,000 tickets is all but impossible for casual fans.

Daytona Beach Practicalities

A world apart from the spring break, biker, and race car scenes, but just a block from the beach, the classic 1950s luncheonette **Bertie's** (2575 N. Atlantic Ave.; 386/672-8656) serves breakfasts and good sandwiches.

Daytona has a lot of low-rise motels, and tons of high-rise hotels along the beachfront, like the large and spacious **Holiday Inn** ($125 and up; 930 N. Atlantic Ave.; 386/255-5494).

The Space Coast: Cape Canaveral

It's more than a little ironic that one of the most extensive sections of natural coastal wetlands left in Florida became home to

Inland from the Space Coast is Florida's biggest tourist attraction, Orlando, home of Walt Disney World. For a Disneyfied view of the ideal American town, visit the Walt Disney Company's very pleasant retro-Victorian planned community of **Celebration** (pop. 11,000 and growing), south of US-192 at the I-4 junction. Contrary to popular belief, this is not the town seen in the Jim Carrey movie *The Truman Show* (that was Seaside, in the Florida Panhandle), but it could have been.

the launch pads of the nation's space program. Though the natural aspects—thousands of seabirds and wide open stretches of sandy beaches—are attractive enough in their own right to merit a visit, many people are drawn here by Cape Canaveral's **Kennedy Space Center.** All the big milestones in the history of the U.S. space program—the Mercury, Gemini, Apollo, and space shuttle launches—happened here, and if names like Alan Shepard, John Glenn, or Neil Armstrong mean anything to you, set aside time for a visit.

The Kennedy Space Center itself, eight miles west of US-1 via the NASA Parkway (Hwy-405), is open to the public, but only on guided tours. These tours require advance tickets, and all leave from the large **visitors complex** (daily; $20–45; 866/737-5235), where two IMAX theaters show films of outer space to get you in the mood. There are also some small museums, a simulated space shuttle mission control center, a half dozen missiles in the Rocket Garden, and an actual space shuttle, which you can walk through. The visitors center also has a couple of fast-food restaurants and a kennel for pets.

To see the Kennedy Space Center up close, board a bus for a tour; these leave every few minutes and visit the Apollo and space shuttle

space shuttle *Endeavor*'s final launch, Cape Canaveral

launch pads and other sites, including a mock-up of the International Space Station. On other tours, you can visit the Cape Canaveral Air Force station or the Cape Canaveral Air Station, site of many early space race adventures, or even

have lunch with an astronaut and talk about outer space with someone who's actually been there (glass of Tang not included).

To watch a rocket launch at Kennedy Space Center, you can get passes from the visitors center, or simply watch from the many good vantage points: Playalinda Beach, in the Canaveral National Seashore at the west end of Hwy-402 from Titusville; across the Indian River, along US-1 in Titusville; or the beaches west of Hwy-A1A in Cocoa Beach.

At the entrance to the Kennedy Space Center visitors center, the **Astronaut Memorial** is a huge black granite block backed by high-tech mirrors that reflect sunlight onto the surface of the stone, illuminating the engraved names of the men and women who have given their lives exploring space.

One of the best places to eat in this part of Florida is west of the Space Center, in the town of Titusville: **Dixie Crossroads** (daily; 1475 Garden St.; 321/268-5000) is an immense (and immensely popular) place to eat seafood, especially massive plates of shrimp. All-you-can-eat piles of small shrimp cost close to $40, while jumbo shrimp cost around $2 apiece. The Crossroads is away from the water, two miles east of I-95 exit 220.

Cocoa Beach

The town of **Cocoa Beach,** familiar to anyone who ever watched the 1960s space age sitcom *I Dream of Jeannie,* sits south of the Kennedy Space Center. Long before there

East from Hwy-A1A on the south side of Cocoa Beach, I Dream of Jeannie Lane leads down to a nice beachfront park.

Detour: Orlando and Walt Disney World

Entire guidebooks are devoted to covering the mind-boggling array of tourist attractions in and around Orlando, but three words would probably suffice: **Walt Disney World.** Over 50,000 people come here every day to experience the magic of the Magic Kingdom, which is divided into four main areas—the Magic Kingdom amusement park, a new Animal Kingdom animal park, the futuristic EPCOT Center, and the Disney-MGM studio tours. Entrance to any of these will set you back around $80; to see all of them, get a Park Hopper pass, which is valid for four days (about $225) or longer. For further information on admissions and lodging packages call 407/824-4321.

At the time of writing, there's still no law that says you have to go to Disney World just because you've come to Florida, but it is a cultural phenomenon and more than a little fun. While you're in Orlando, you may want to visit other big-time attractions like Sea World and Universal Studios, but there are also some funky, pre-Disney-era tourist traps, with ad budgets small enough that you won't have to fight the crowds. Best of this bunch is probably **GatorLand** (daily; $24; 14501 S. Orange Blossom Trail; 407/855-5496), where thousands of alligators, crocodiles, snakes, and other reptiles are gathered together in a cypress swamp. You enter through a gator's gaping jaws, and inside you can see such sights as live chickens being dangled

were space shuttles, or even NASA, Cocoa Beach was home to the Cape Canaveral Air Station, the launch site for the unmanned space probes of the late 1950s, including the first U.S. satellite (Explorer 1), and the famous "astro chimps" (Gordo, Able, and Miss Baker, who were sent into orbit to test the effects of weightlessness). The air station, which is accessible through the Kennedy Space Center complex, has historical exhibits and dozens of missiles, from today's Patriots back to German V2s (which were fired at England during World War II and provided the engineering basis for the American rockets of a decade later). The on-site museum includes early computers and other equipment,

over a pond, taunting the hungry carnivorous gators just of out reach below. Continuing south along US-441, past the world headquarters of Tupperware, another sight of offbeat interest is the 100-year-old historic district at the heart of **Kissimmee** (pop. 38,200), where a 50-foot stone and concrete pyramid, constructed in 1943 with rocks from most states, as well as 21 countries, stands in Lake Front Park.

The entertaining design of Disney World doesn't stop at the park gates. *Au contraire.* Perhaps the most memorable aspect of the Disney experience is seeing how the clever folks at Disney deal with "real life," specifically the lodging, dining, shopping, and entertainment options around the park. It doesn't take a Boy Genius to figure out the customer base of Disney World's Jimmy Neutron–themed **Nickelodeon Family Suites** ($125 and up; 877/642-5111), a kid-friendly Holiday Inn with multiple bedroom suites (and a fun but chaotic pool area—avoid the holiday peak times) near Disney World. Another movie spinoff is Disney's extraordinary **Animal Kingdom Lodge** (around $250; 407/939-6244), where a 30-acre savannah landscape, complete with roaming giraffes and zebras you can see from your balconies, offers families and fans of *The Lion King* the chance to take an African safari—without the jet lag. And it's not all just for little kids: sports fans flock to the **All Star Sports Resort,** a sports-themed hotel next to the ESPN/ABC Wide World of Sports complex, spring training home of the Atlanta Braves.

Between Orlando and the Space Coast, the Beeline Expressway (Hwy-528) is a fast, flat toll road, with only three exits in the 30 miles between I-95 and greater Orlando.

housed inside the blockhouse from which the first launches were controlled.

Though space travel is clearly on the minds of many residents, especially personnel stationed at Patrick Air Force Base here, another focus is catching the perfect wave: Cocoa Beach is surf center of the Space Coast. Along with a clean, 10-mile-long beach, the town also holds a batch of good-value motels, located within a short walk of the waves. Choose from chains (including a Motel 6), or check out the garish pink **Fawlty Towers** ($85 and up; 100 E. Cocoa Beach Causeway/ Hwy-520; 321/784-3870), which for fans of the eponymous British sit-com is sadly devoid of John Cleese or put-upon Juan.

It is
the
to
the
(41
888
and
boa

Ve

As
un
dis
the
L.
wh
of
D
wh
se
D
D
ne

w
P
ab
st
er
p
D
h
v

F

S
H
(
o
i
d
I
A

South of Fort Pierce, Port St. Lucie is the spring training home of the New York Mets (525 NW Peacock Blvd., off I-95; 772/871-2115).

Midway between Jupiter and Palm Beach, the hamlet of **Juno Beach** is home to the entertaining and educational **Loggerhead Marinelife Center** (14200 US-1; 561/627-8280).

of the region, showing off a hand-carved canoe and explaining the "fort" in Fort Pierce (it was built in 1835, during the Seminole Wars).

Heading south from Fort Pierce, Hwy-A1A embarks on a nearly 30-mile run along Hutchinson Island, where dense stands of pines block the views of largely undeveloped beachfront. On the coast just north of Palm Beach, the town of **Jupiter** has a landmark lighthouse, which you can climb inside up to the top for a grand view, and Roger Dean Stadium is spring training home of the Marlins and Cardinals, as well as their Class A Florida League farm clubs. Pop culture fans may also want to know that Jupiter has long been home to movie star Burt Reynolds: His achievements (from TV's *Gunsmoke* through movies like *Deliverance* and *Smokey and the Bandit*) are chronicled at his acting school and museum (Thurs.–Sun.; $5; 100 N. US-1; 561/743-9955), though redevelopment threatens to leave Burt's museum and school without a home.

Palm Beach

A South Florida sibling to the conspicuous consumption that once defined Newport, Rhode Island, **Palm Beach** (pop. 10,468) has been a winter refuge for the rich and famous since Henry Flagler started work on his fashionable (but long-vanished) resort hotel, the 1,150-room Royal Poinciana. It was the world's largest wood building when completed in 1894, but the site is now an upscale shopping district at the center of town. Away from here, most of Palm Beach is well-guarded private property, off-limits to most mere mortals. The best way for anyone not named Kennedy or Pierpont to get a look at Palm Beach life is to spend some time at the Hearst Castle of the East Coast, the **Henry Morrison Flagler Museum** (closed Mon.; $18; 561/655-2833), on the inland side of downtown Palm Beach, at the north end of Cocoanut Row. Officially known as Whitehall, this opulent 60,000-square-foot

> Inland from Palm Beach, you can wave at rhinos, lions, and wildebeests in a 500-acre, drive-through simulation of African ecosystems at **Lion Country Safari** ($28; 561/793-1084), 18 miles west of I-95 via US-98. No convertibles allowed!

mansion was Flagler's private home, and the 50-plus rooms (many of which were taken from European buildings and re-installed here) contain historical exhibits tracing the life of Flagler, the Standard Oil baron (John D. Rockefeller's right-hand man) who made a fortune while making Florida into an immensely popular vacation destination.

Not surprisingly, there are some very good and very expensive restaurants in and around Palm Beach, but happily there's also a very nice, normal, all-American luncheonette just two blocks north of The Breakers: **Green's Pharmacy** (151 N. County Rd.; 561/832- 0304) serves very good diner-style meals.

Even bigger and better than Whitehall is **The Breakers,** a stately resort hotel that faces the ocean at the east end of Palm Beach and retains much of its 1920s Mediterranean style and grace. Rooms will set you back around $350 a night (much more for suites), but you can enjoy the lobby, have a drink or afternoon tea, or take a tour (Wed. at 3 PM only; free; 561/655-6611).

Boca Raton

Whoever named **Boca Raton** (pop. 84,392), which translates literally as "Rat's Mouth," clearly didn't have an ear for future promotional bonanza, but despite the awkward name the town has become one of the more chichi spots in the state. As in Palm Beach, Coral Gables, and Miami's South Beach, the best of Boca dates from the 1920s, when architect and real estate promoter Addison Mizner, flush from his success building Mediterranean-style manors in Palm Beach, created a mini Venice of resorts and canals, which survives mainly in the shocking pink palazzo of the **Boca Raton Resort** ($200 and up; 501 E. Camino Real; 561/447-3000), on the southeast side of town.

Downtown Boca has been turned into a massive stucco shopping mall, but it's worth braving for a look inside the ornate Mizner-designed Town Hall, on US-1 (old Dixie Highway) in Palmetto Park downtown, which now houses the local historical museum (closed Mon.; free).

US-1, the main route through town, also holds the very popular **Boca Diner** (2801 N. Federal Hwy.; 561/750-6744), serving above-average coffee shop fare; the early evening early-bird scene here is straight out of *Seinfeld*. Boca Raton is also home to one of the best sushi places in South Florida: **Daimatsu,** in the heart of Boca's downtown shopping district (271 SE Mizner Blvd.; 561/361-7557).

Hwy-A1A misses most of Boca Raton, cruising past along the densely pine-forested coast. The beaches are accessible but hard to find; one well-marked stop along the way is the **Gumbo Limbo Nature Center** (Mon.–Sat. 9 AM–4 PM, Sun. noon–4 PM; $5 donation; 561/338-1473) on the inland side of the highway, a mile north of Mizner Park. A variety of native Floridian landscapes have been re-created here, letting you wander at will past coastal dunes, mangrove wetlands, and rare sabal palm hammocks. Across Hwy-A1A, **Red Reef Park** is a popular surfing beach.

Fort Lauderdale

Once famed for wild spring break frolics that saw thousands of college kids descending here for an orgy of drunken round-the-clock partying, **Fort Lauderdale** (pop. 165,651) is a surprisingly residential city, brought to a more human scale by

Fort Lauderdale

the many waterways that cut through it. One of the largest cargo ports in the state, Fort Lauderdale also boasts more boats per capita than just about anywhere else in the United States, and over 165 miles of canals, inlets, and other waterways flow through the city.

Fort Lauderdale is said to be one of the points that form the Bermuda Triangle, so of course there are numerous beachside bars where college kids try to simulate its supernatural effects by imbibing too many margaritas.

Downtown Fort Lauderdale has a few big, dull office towers, but along the New River there are some well-preserved historic buildings dating back to 1905, when the city first emerged from the swamps. Find out more by visiting the **Fort Lauderdale History Center** (Tues.–Sun. noon–4 PM; $10; 231 SW 2nd Ave.), west of US-1, which has lots of old photos and walking-tour maps, or the nifty **Stranahan House** (daily; $12; 335 SE 6th Ave.), off Las Olas Boulevard. This circa-1901 trading post and home, with broad verandas and high ceilings,is one of the most evocative historic places in the state.

Fort Lauderdale's main beachfront bar and nightclub district is along Atlantic Avenue and Las Olas Boulevard, where you'll find some nice sidewalk cafés and fast-food restaurants. One culinary landmark is **Johnny V.'s** (625 E. Las Olas; 954/761-7920), a popular and stylish haunt where traditional American dishes are enlivened by a canny blend of exotic ingredients. For a change of pace from the frenetic tourism, or simply to enjoy good basic fried seafood, cold beer, and live blues, head south down US-1 to **Ernie's BBQ Lounge** (1843 S. Federal Hwy.; 954/523-8636), famous for its conch fritters, calamari rings, and rooftop deck.

Miles of inexpensive motels line Hwy-A1A north of Fort Lauderdale, and unless there's something big going on you shouldn't have trouble finding a room for under $100—half that in summer. One of the nicest places is the moderately priced, family-friendly **TropiRock Resort** ($80 and up; 2900 Belmar St.; 954/564-0523), with tennis courts, a tiki bar, and a pool, just a short walk from the beach.

North of Fort Lauderdale, Hwy-A1A winds in along the coast through a series of funky, friendly beachside communities. South of Fort Lauderdale, Hwy-A1A heads inland and merges into US-1, returning to the coast for the run south to Miami Beach.

North Miami Beach

Between Fort Lauderdale and Miami Beach, Hwy-A1A runs along the shore, first as Ocean Drive and later as Collins Avenue, while US-1 runs inland parallel to (and sometimes as) the old Dixie Highway. There's nothing here to compare with the attractions farther south, but the town of **North Miami Beach** does have one oddity: the **Ancient Spanish Monastery** (hours vary; $8; 16711 W. Dixie Hwy.; 305/945-1461), a 12th-century monastery bought in the 1920s by William Randolph Hearst, who had it dismantled and shipped to the United States for his Hearst Castle complex in California. However, after the stones were confiscated by U.S. Customs and Hearst lost his fortune in the Great Depression, the monastery was finally rebuilt here in Florida—as an Episcopal church.

On the coast, Hwy-A1A runs past a number of indistinct beach towns before hitting **Bal Harbour,** home to one of Miami's biggest and best shopping malls, and one of its biggest beaches, **Haulover Beach.** Besides having a café, lots of tennis courts, and gorgeous sands, Haulover Beach is also famous for attracting the clothing-optional crowd.

From Haulover Beach south to Miami Beach, Collins Avenue (Hwy-A1A) used to be known as "Millionaire's Row" for all the huge estates here, but now the road is lined with towering concrete condos and hotels, including the landmark Morris Lapidus–designed complex of the **Fontainebleau Resort** ($200 and up; 4441 Collins Ave.; 305/538-2000). It's been the setting for several movies: Jerry Lewis filmed *The Bellboy* here in 1959; Sean Connery checked in as James Bond, most famously in the film *Goldfinger;* and Al Pacino hung out by the pool in the quintessential 1980s Miami movie, *Scarface.*

Miami Beach

Covering a broad island separating downtown Miami from the open Atlantic Ocean, **Miami Beach** (pop. 84,633) has long been a mecca for fans of 1930s art deco architecture and design. More recently, it's also become one of the world's most fashionable and bacchanalian beach resorts, with deluxe hotels and high-style nightclubs and restaurants lining the broad white sands of South Beach, the relatively small corner of Miami Beach

The stately Mediterranean Revival manor where fashion designer Gianni Versace lived and was murdered sits at the heart of South Beach, on Ocean Drive just north of 11th Street.

Carl Fisher: Father of Miami Beach

Fisher Park, on the bay side of Miami Beach on Alton Road at 51st Street, holds a small monument to the fascinating Carl Fisher, the man most responsible for turning Miami Beach from a mangrove swamp into America's favorite resort. Before building up Lincoln Avenue into Miami Beach's first commercial district, Carl Fisher had played an important role in America's early automotive history. Called the "P. T. Barnum of the Automobile Age," Fisher made millions through the Prest-O-Lite company, which in the early 1900s developed the first functioning car headlight. Around 1910, he invested this fortune in building and promoting the Indianapolis Motor Speedway, then went on to plan and publicize both the Lincoln Highway, America's first transcontinental road, and the Dixie Highway, the first main north—south route in the eastern United States. He invested heavily in Miami Beach property but was ruined by the Great Depression and the sudden drop in land values. He died here, nearly penniless, in 1939, just as the economy was rebounding and the art deco hotels of South Beach were bringing new life to Miami Beach.

that gets 99 percent of the press and tourist attention. Here, along beachfront Ocean Drive and busier Collins Avenue (Hwy-A1A) a block inland, you'll find dozens of glorious art deco hotels, many lighted with elegant neon signs. Guided walking tours (daily; $20) of the district leave from the **Art Deco Welcome Center** (daily; 1001 Ocean Dr.; 305/672-2014), which also rents iPod-based self-guided tours and sells guidebooks, posters, postcards, and anything else you can think of that has to do with the art deco era.

No matter how intoxicating the architecture, beach life, and nightlife along South Beach are, while you're here be sure to set aside an hour or two to explore the fascinating

Miami

Equal parts jet-set glitz and multicultural grit, and with more than half its population coming here from other countries around the globe, Miami (pop. 435,000) really embodies the transitive state of the nation in the early years of the 21st century. Having sprung up from swampland in the 1920s, Miami has weathered hurricanes and race riots, real estate booms and busts, drug running, and endless political intrigue to become one of America's most energetic cities. In her 1987 book *Miami*, Joan Didion describes the city as an economically schizophrenic place where it's possible "to pass from walled enclaves to utter desolation while changing stations on the car radio."

Approaching from Miami Beach past the cruise ship docks along the MacArthur Causeway, or the older and more leisurely Venetian Causeway, you experience the view of Miami made famous by the 1980s television series *Miami Vice*—downtown towers rising above Biscayne Bay. West of downtown, Miami's most engaging district is Little Havana, which focuses along SW 8th Street (a.k.a. Calle Ocho) between 12th and 16th Avenues. Since the 1950s and 1960s, when the first refugees fleeing Castro's regime fetched up here, this neighborhood has been the heart of Cuban-American Miami. Hang out for a while with the old men who congregate in the Domino Park on 8th Street and 14th Avenue, or visit the Martyrs of Giron (a.k.a. Bay of

collection of pop culture artifacts on display two blocks inland at the **Wolfsonian** (closed Wed.; $5; 1001 Washington Ave.; 305/531-1001). One of the odder highbrow museums you'll find, the Wolfsonian (officially the Mitchell Wolfson Jr. Collection of Decorative and Propaganda Arts) fills a retrofitted 1920s warehouse with four floors of furniture, sculpture, architectural models, posters, and much more, almost all dating from the "Modern Era," roughly 1885 to 1945. Two areas of excellence are drawings and murals created under the New Deal auspices of the WPA, and similar agitprop artifacts created in Weimar, Germany. Only a small portion of the extensive collection is on display at any one time, and most of the floor space is given over to changing exhibitions—on anything from World's Fairs to Florida tourism to how children's books were used to indoctrinate future soldiers—but it's a

Beach; it h
is now pac
refinement
Samba Dr
ers' paradi:

Across I

The I-95 f
Miami no
neighborh
crosses Bis
Biscayne E
historic B
bank and
way systen
then sout
Highway
the Florida

Coral Ga

South of
neighborl
grand gat
(8th Stree
of **Coral**
Florida re
fairly und
years of tl
vards, fine
mark to lc
up; 1200
off Grana
in 1926 ai
(Johnny V
stored to i
  The sou
campus o
US-1, the

Homest

One of tl
Florida Kc
Dixie Hw

Pigs) Monument along 8th Street between 12th and 13th Streets; you'll definitely get a feel for it. Better yet, stop for something to eat or drink at one of Little Havana's many great Cuban cafés, like **Versailles** (3555 SW 8th St.; 305/444-0240), a favorite haunt of Miami's politically potent anti-Castro Cuban-Americans. Enjoy very good, very traditional Cuban food: toasted chorizo sandwiches, or perhaps a bowl of *ropa vieja* (tender threads of garlicky beef in a black bean soup), finished off with a creamy flan and a cup of super-strong Cuban coffee.

For an entirely different aspect of Miami, check out the two-time wild card World Series champion **Florida Marlins** (305/930-4487), who play at the retractably roofed $700 million stadium on the site of the historic Orange Bowl.

Miami Beach has the best range of stylish hotels, but in downtown Miami the characterful and historic **Miami River Inn** is a well-preserved circa-1908 hotel with B&B rooms (all with private baths) in a slightly dodgy downtown neighborhood ($70–199; 118 SW South River Dr.; 305/325-0045). At the top end of the style and expense spectrum is the **Four Seasons** ($350 and up; 1435 Brickell Ave.; 305/358-3535), offering stunning views from a 64-story tower. Back down to earth, the major chains all have locations on the downtown waterfront; as at all South Florida accommodations, room rates tend to increase considerably during the peak season (Jan.–Apr.).

The best source of information on greater Miami, including Miami Beach, is the **Greater Miami visitors bureau** (701 Brickell Ave.; 305/539-3000 or 800/933-8448).

thought-provoking and surprisingly fun place, with an unexpressed but overriding theme of how art can counterbalance, or at least respond to, the demands of industrial society.

Miami Beach Practicalities

Not surprisingly, there are scores of cafés and restaurants in and around Miami Beach; some, like exotic **Wish** (801 Collins Ave.; 305/531-2222) in The Hotel, are rated among the best in the world. More down to earth, and just two blocks west of the beach, the **11th Street Diner** (305/534-6373) on 11th and Washington is a 1948 Paramount pre-fab diner, plunked down in 1992 and open 24 hours ever since.

For an unforgettably hedonistic experience, check into one of South Beach's great old art deco hotels, or at least saunter through the lobby and stop for a drink. The **Delano** ($350

and u
Ave.; :
high-si
symph
the **R**
up; 17
305/5:
cooles
Beach
ally sa
out alc

The
influei
evident e
go, but f
how deep t
run, consid
two of (
presi
Machado
Socarra
Miami's
Cemet(
of Little I
Nicar
Anast
bu

Key
We

© AVALON TRA

out of huge blocks of oolitic coral in the 1930s. Located right along the highway, two miles north of Homestead, the house is filled with furniture also carved from stone—a 3,000-pound sofa and a 500-pound rocking chair—and no one has figured how its enigmatic creator (Ed Leedskalnin) did it all without help or the use of any heavy machinery.

Homestead, along with neighboring Florida City farther south, forms the main gateway to Everglades National Park, and there are tons of reasonably priced motels hereabouts— all the usual suspects line up here along US-1, including the very nice **Best Western Gateway to the Keys** ($90 and up; 305/246-5100).

Florida's other big national park, **Biscayne National Park,** stretches east of Homestead from near Miami to the top of the Florida Keys, but it is almost completely underwater. Privately run snorkeling and diving tours (around $30–35) leave from near the main **Convoy Point visitors center** (305/230-7275), nine miles east of US-1 at the end of 328th Street—near the huge Homestead-Miami Speedway (and a nuclear power plant).

Everglades National Park

Covering over 1.5 million acres at the far southwestern tip of mainland Florida, **Everglades National Park** protects the largest subtropical wilderness in the United States. A fair portion of the park is actually underwater, and the entire Everglades ecosystem is basically a giant, slow-flowing river that is 50 miles wide but only a few inches deep. Fed by Lake Okeechobee, and under constant threat by irrigation in-flows and out-flows and by the redirection of water to Miami and other cities, the Everglades still seem to vibrate with life. Some 300 species of birds breed here, as do 600 different kinds of fish and animals, ranging from rare manatees to abundant alligators (not to mention the gazillions of mosquitoes).

The backcountry parts of the Everglades can be visited by boat, but by road there are

the observation tower in Shark Valley

only two main routes. In the north, the Tamiami Trail (the Tampa to Miami Trail, a.k.a. US-41) heads west from Miami to misnamed **Shark Valley,** where you can rent bikes or take a tram tour ($18.50 for tram tour, $7.50 per hour for bike rentals, $10 entrance fee) on a 15-mile loop through the sawgrass swamps that make up the heart of the Everglades. Gazing at the gators, eagles, and hawks here, it's hard to believe you're barely a half hour from South Beach. Just west of

Gators!

Shark Valley, the **Miccosukee Indian Village** is a somewhat poignant reminder of the plight of the Everglades native peoples, the Seminoles, whose ancestors fought off the U.S. Army but who now wrestle alligators, run casinos and souvenir shops, and give airboat tours of their ancestral lands.

The main road access to the Everglades is via Palm Drive (Hwy-9336) from the Florida Turnpike or US-1. This route takes you past the **Ernest Coe Visitors Center** (305/242-7700), where interpretive displays and a pair of nature trails give an appetizing taste of the

In the Everglades, and anywhere in Florida, mosquitoes are intensely annoying pests, so if you're here at any time but the dry middle of winter, bring strong insect repellent—and lots of it. In parts of the Everglades, the bugs are so bad that full-body cover is recommended, in addition to the most potent sprays and lotions you can lay your hands on.

Everglades (and almost guaranteed sightings of alligators). The road continues nearly 40 miles west to the former town of Flamingo, where both the residents and the namesake birds have all moved on, and the Everglades' only eating and accommodation option, the Flamingo Lodge, closed after suffering damage in the 2005 Katrina hurricane.

Key Largo

The Overseas Highway (US-1) officially starts in Florida City, near the Everglades some 50 miles south of Miami, but doesn't really come alive until it leaves the mainland

The Overseas Highway

Imagine a narrow ribbon of asphalt and concrete hovering between emerald seas and azure blue skies, and lined by swaying palm trees and gorgeous, white-sand beaches. Add a generous taste of exotic wildlife, including alligators and dolphins; the country's only tropical coral reefs; and a romantic history rich with tales of buccaneering pirates and buried treasure. Hang it off the far southern tip of Florida, and you have the Overseas Highway, one of the country's most fascinating scenic drives.

Running for over 125 miles from the Everglades to the edge of the Caribbean, the Overseas Highway is the southernmost section of US-1, the historic route that winds for over 2,400 miles along the full length of the East Coast. From its very inception, the Overseas Highway has been unique. It was built on top of the legendary Florida and East Coast Railroad, which at the turn of the 20th century linked the great resort hotels of St. Augustine and Palm Beach with Key West and Cuba. An engineering masterpiece, the railroad cost $50 million and hundreds of lives to complete in 1912, but it lasted only two decades before the century's most powerful hurricane destroyed the tracks in September 1935. The state of Florida bought the remnants of the railroad for $650,000 and proceeded to convert it into a two-lane highway, the Overseas

and lands at **Key Largo,** the first and largest of the dozens of "keys" (from the Spanish word *cayos,* meaning small islands) the highway links together. The Overseas Highway reaches Key Largo at the very popular **John Pennekamp Coral Reef State Park** (daily; $8; MM 102.5; 305/451-1202). The first place where you can really get a feel for life on the keys, the park is the starting point for a variety of **guided tours** (scuba diving, snorkeling, or in glass-bottomed boats) that offer up-close looks at

Between milemarker 106 and milemarker 86, a hiking and bicycling path parallels US-1—sometimes very closely—but it's a rare long-distance route on these tiny islands.

Highway, which opened to traffic in 1938. Most of the old road has since been superseded by a more modern highway, but many old bridges and causeways still stand as evocative remnants of an earlier era.

As in much of Florida, ramshackle roadside development has uglified much of the route—in the larger keys towns, like Key Largo, Islamorada, and Marathon, signs hawking restaurants, motels, and snorkel tours are more common than pelicans—but you can't help but be hypnotized by the scenic beauty of what pockets of nature still remain. Many of the best views are from the road itself, and specifically from the bridges, such as the Long Key Bridge and soaring Seven Mile Bridge, which run north and south of Marathon. Two state parks, John Pennecamp on Key Largo and Bahia Honda in the Lower Keys, offer a respite from the commercialism, and all along the Overseas Highways, unmarked roads and driveways lead across the narrow keys down to the water side, where all manner of sportfishing marinas and Margaritaville-type bars give you another outlook on the true "key experience."

All the way along the Overseas Highway (US-1), the roadside is lined by milemarker (MM) posts counting down the miles from Florida City to Key West, starting at MM 127 and ending up at MM 0; addresses usually make reference to these numbers. Though it's only about 160 miles, be sure to allow at least four hours for the drive between Miami and Key West—plus however many hours you manage to spend out of the car, of course.

the only tropical coral reef in the continental United States and all but guarantee that you'll see enough sealife to fill a photo album or two. Along with the adjacent **Key Largo Coral Reef National Marine Sanctuary,** the park gives access to more than 175 square miles of diving spots, including reefs, shipwrecks, and a nine-foot-high bronze statue called *Christ of the Deep.* The visitors center has a replica reef in a 30,000-gallon aquarium full of colorful fish, allowing a quick look at the fascinating underwater world without getting your feet wet; the park also has other on-land attractions, like a boardwalk over a mangrove swamp and a pleasant campground.

Key Largo is home to the **Key Lime Products** store (305/853-0378) at milemarker 95, selling all manner of key lime pies, juice, cakes, cookies, suntan lotions—even key lime trees, though commercial key lime orchards are a thing of the past. (Most key limes today come from Mexico and Honduras.)

Film fans will know that Key Largo was the title and setting of a great 1948 film noir movie starring Bogie, Bacall, and Edward G. Robinson; these days, it's also home to the co-star of another classic, the boat from the *African Queen,* which is moored next to the Holiday Inn at milemarker 100. Most of Key Largo today, however, is a rather tawdry four-mile stretch of seashell stands, dive shops, boat shops, and margarita bars; there are many good restaurants, including **Mrs. Mac's Kitchen** (closed Sun.; MM 99.4; 305/451-3722), a small and friendly place with inexpensive food and more beers to drink than seats to sit on.

Key Largo also has many good places to stay, from the funky **Sunset Cove Motel** ($115 and up; MM 99.5; 305/451-0705) to the boutique **Azul del Mar** ($175 and up; MM 104.3; 305/451-0337), a relaxing small resort. Also here is the unique **Jules' Undersea Lodge** (packages from $250 per person; 305/451-2353), a two-room motel that's 22 feet beneath the sea—a quick scuba dive down from 51 Shoreland Drive, off MM 103.2.

Islamorada

Continuing south on US-1, Key Largo blends into **Islamorada** (pronounced "EYE-la-mo-RA-da"), the self-proclaimed "Sportfishing Capital of the World," where anglers from all over the world come to try their hand at catching the elusive, hard-fighting bonefish that dwell in the shallow saltwater "flats" and the deep-sea tarpon, marlin, and sailfish. Though now famous for its fishing and fun-in-the-sun, Islamorada (Purple Island) used to be synonymous with death and destruction: On September 2, 1935, a huge tidal wave, whipped up by 200-mile-per-hour hurricane winds, drowned over 400 veterans and local residents trying to escape on what turned out

Entering Islamorada from the north, you are welcomed to town by the "World's Largest Lobster," standing at milemarker 86.1 in front of the Rain Barrel Artisan Village. She hasn't yet been boiled or grilled, so she's a naturally green-brown color, not bright red.

to be the last train ever to travel along the old Florida East Coast Railway. Most of the dead were World War I veterans, members of the "Bonus Army" who had marched on Washington, D.C., in 1934 and had been given jobs working to build the Overseas Highway. A stone pillar at the south end of Islamorada, along US-1 at milemarker 81.6, was erected by the WPA to remember the event.

At the center of Islamorada sits one of the older tourist traps in south Florida: the **Theater of the Sea** (daily; $26.95; MM 84.5; 305/664-2431), a funky, friendly place where you can watch performing sea animals or even swim with dolphins.

Islamorada is also home to what may be the most pleasant and plushest accommodation option in the Florida Keys: **The Moorings** ($250 and up; 123 Beach Rd.; 305/664-4708), on the ocean side of milemarker 81.5. The Moorings is an idyllic and much-loved retreat, with 18 self-sufficient wooden cottages on 18 acres, alongside a beautiful 1,100-foot white-sand beach.

The Moorings also has a nice restaurant, **Morada Bay** (81600 Overseas Hwy.; 305/664-0604), serving urbane renditions of traditional key favorites on US-1 at milemarker 81.6. For a more down-to-earth taste of the keys, try the nearby **Green Turtle Inn** (closed Mon.; 305/664-2006), where specialties include shrimp 'n' grits and local fish.

For more information on Islamorada, stop by the little red caboose that holds the **visitors bureau** (MM 82.5; 305/664-4503 or 800/322-5397). Outside, in the parking lot, informational plaques tell the story of the ill-fated railroad that became the Overseas Highway.

Long Key State Park

South of Islamorada, up and over the high "Channel 5" bridge, the roadside scene gets pretty again very fast, especially at the **Long Key State Park** at milemarker 67.5, where boardwalks wind through coastal hammocks (dense stands of mahogany and dogwood trees that bunch together on the small humps of land that lie above the tide line). There's a campground ($36; 305/664-4815) in the park, with showers, and some nice but narrow beaches.

Marathon and Pigeon Key

The second-longest of the many bridges that make up US-1, the elegant multi-arched Long Key Bridge supports a long,

flat causeway where the
road finally earns its
other name, the Overseas
Highway. Unobstructed
views of the distant ho-
rizon are yours in all directions, with the narrow
ribbon of highway seem-
ingly suspended between

the sky and the sea. Fortunately, turnouts at both ends of the
causeway let you take in the vista without worrying about on-
coming traffic.

The Long Key Bridge marks the northern end of **Marathon,**
a sprawling community that's the second largest in the keys,
stretching between milemarkers 65 and 47 over a series of islands. One of the visitor highlights of Marathon is on Grassy
Key, where the **Dolphin Research Center** (daily; $19.50; MM
59; 305/289-0002), a rest home for dolphins who've been kept
in captivity for too long, is marked by a 30-foot-tall statue of a
leaping dolphin. You can swim with a dolphin for around $175.

Accessible by tram from a visitors center in Marathon,
Pigeon Key (daily; $11; MM 48; 305/743-5999) is one of
the least famous but perhaps most fascinating spots along
the Overseas Highway. A national historic district, preserving substantial remnants of the clapboard construction camp
that housed some 400 workers employed on the original
Seven Mile Bridge from 1912 to 1935, Pigeon Key offers a
glimpse of blue-collar keys history the likes of which you'll
find nowhere else.

Lower Keys: Bahia Honda

The old Seven Mile Bridge, which carried first the railroad
and later US-1 over Pigeon Key between Marathon and Big
Pine Key, was replaced in the early 1980s by a soaring new
bridge that gives another batch of breathtaking ocean-to-
gulf views. (The old bridge, which was seen in the Arnold
Schwarzenegger/Jamie Lee Curtis movie *True Lies,* still stands
below the new one but is now used as a very long fishing pier.)

The south end of the Seven Mile Bridge, near milemarker
40, marks the start of the Lower Keys, which are considerably
less commercial than the others. The best of the Lower Keys is
yours to enjoy at milemarker 36.5, where the entrance to **Bahia
Honda State Park** (305/872-2353) leaves the highway behind

and brings you back to the way the keys used to be: covered in palms and coastal hardwood hammocks, with white-sand beaches stretching for miles along blue-water seas. Facilities are limited to a few cabins (around $122.50 off season, $162.50 peak season), a general store, and a snorkel rental stand, but it's a great place to spend some time fishing, beachcombing, sunbathing, or swimming in the deep, warm waters of the Atlantic Ocean or Gulf of Mexico. Camping overnight, the best way to enjoy the sunset, sunrise, and everything in between, costs around $38.50 a night.

From Bahia Honda, US-1 bends along to Big Pine Key, second largest of the keys and suffering from a bout of suburban mini mall sprawl. Though it looks about as far from natural as can be, Big Pine Key happens to be part of the **National Key Deer Refuge,** set up to protect the increasingly

On Bahia Honda Key, near milemarker 37, you can see a double-decker remnant of the original keys railroad, with the 1938 Overseas Highway supported atop the trestle. Widening the rail bed to accommodate cars was impossible, so a new deck was added to the top of the bridge.

white sands, clear water, blue skies: Bahia Honda State Park

po' boys, fresh mahi fish-and-chips, cold beer, and frequent live blues bands make this a great place to soak up Key West's party-hardy-at-the-end-of-the-world ambience.

Where would you like to go? A sign at Key West Marina on Duval Street gives directions and distances to dozens of places around the world.

The **Southernmost Motel in the USA** ($95 and up; 1319 Duval St.; 305/296-6577) has a poolside bar and AAA-rated rooms. A surprisingly desirable option is the **Crowne Plaza** ($150 and up; 430 Duval St.; 305/296-2991), which plasters its chain-hotel name on the facade of the La Concha Hotel, one of Key West's oldest and largest hotels, but otherwise preserves the historic 1920s character; you can't get more central than this. There are also many nice old B&Bs around Key West, like the landmark **Old Town Manor** ($150 and up; 511 Eaton St.; 305/292-2170), an 1880s Greek Revival mansion with a gorgeous garden.

The official end of US-1 is marked by a zero milepost sign in front of the Key West post office, on Truman Avenue.

Key West is the end of the Overseas Highway, but it's not the end of the sightseeing opportunities, so if you don't want to turn around and head home just yet, you don't have to. You can board a sunset cruise, or take a seaplane tour of historic **Fort Jefferson,** a photogenic 150-year-old fortress and prison located on an island in **Dry Tortugas National Park,** 68 miles west of Key West. Prisoners held here included the hapless doctor Samuel Mudd, who set the broken leg of Lincoln assassin John Wilkes Booth.

Index

Photo and Illustration Credits

Road Trip USA and the Moon logo are the property of Avalon Travel, a member of the Perseus Books Group. All other photos, marks and logos depicted are the property of the original owners. All rights reserved.

All vintage postcards, photographs and maps in this book from the private collection of Jamie Jensen, unless otherwise credited. Photos © Jamie Jensen: pages 62 and 110.

United States Quarter-Dollar Coin Images

State quarter-dollar coin images from the United States Mint. Used with permission.

United States Postage Stamps

All postage stamps © United States Postal Service. All rights reserved. Used with permission. Written authorization from the Postal Service is required to use, reproduce, post, transmit, distribute, or publicly display these images. Pages 6, 18, 49, 72, 77 Greetings from America Series Stamp Designs © 2002 United States Postal Service

Minor League Baseball Logos

All Minor League Baseball logos are Registered Trademarks of their organizations. Used with permission. Pages 32, 51, 67, 90.

The following images were sourced from www.123rf.com:

10 © P. Orbital, 30 © Tom McNemar, 75 (top) © Iofoto, 75 (bottom) © Carolina K. Smith, M.D., 81 (top) © Rui Dios Aidos, 92 © Ivan Cholakov, 100 © William Silver, 101 © Oleg Zinkovetsky, 107 (top) © Natalia Bratslavsky, 107 (bottom) © Varina and Jay Patel, 110 (top) © Chris Cifatte.

State flag images:

© Juergen Priewe at www.123rf.com, pages 21, 25, 32, 62.

Public Domain images:

The following images are in the public domain because one of the following applies:
* The work is a work of a U.S. government soldier or employee, taken or made during the course of the person's official duties. As a work of the U.S. federal government, the image is in the public domain.
* The work was published in the United States between 1923 and 1977 and without a copyright notice. Unless its author has been dead for several years, it is copyrighted in jurisdictions that do not apply the rule of the shorter term for US works, such as Canada (50 p.m.a.), Mainland China (50 p.m.a., not Hong Kong or Macao), Germany (70 p.m.a.), Mexico (100 p.m.a.), Switzerland (70 p.m.a.), and other countries with individual treaties.
* The copyright has expired, often because the first publication of the image occurred prior to January 1, 1923.
* The copyright holder of the work has released the work into the public domain. This applies worldwide. In some countries this may not be legally possible; if so: The copyright holder grants anyone the right to use the work for any purpose, without any conditions, unless such conditions are required by law.
* The work is a postage stamp published before 1978.
See http://copyright.cornell.edu/resources/publicdomain.cfm for further explanation.

2 (right) digital file Courtesy Domini Dragoone, 3 (left) digital file Courtesy of Downtowngal/Wikimedia Commons 23 (bottom) Courtesy Tex Jobe, U.S. Army Corps of Engineers/Wikimedia Commons; 27 (bottom) Courtesy United States Coast Guard, PA2 Christopher Evanson; 31 (stamp) Courtesy of the United States Postal Service; 33 (top) Courtesy Library of

Ready to hit the open road?

Visit roadtripusa.com for trip ideas, maps, road trip routes, a Driver's Almanac of monthly trip suggestions, and more.

Web-exclusive features include Jamie Jensen's Road Tripper blog and free downloadable podcasts.

roadtripusa.com—the online source for road trippers!

www.moon.com

DESTINATIONS | ACTIVITIES | BLOGS | MAPS | BOOKS

MOON.COM is ready to help plan your next trip! Filled with fresh trip ideas and strategies, author interviews, informative travel blogs, a detailed map library, and descriptions of all the Moon guidebooks, Moon.com is all you need to get out and explore the world—or even places in your own backyard. While at Moon.com, sign up for our monthly e-newsletter for updates on new releases, travel tips, and expert advice from our on-the-go Moon authors. As always, when you travel with Moon, expect an experience that is uncommon and truly unique.

f 🐦 KEEP UP WITH MOON ON FACEBOOK AND TWITTER
JOIN THE MOON PHOTO GROUP ON FLICKR

ROAD TRIP USA
Atlantic Coast
2nd Edition

Jamie Jensen

Avalon Travel
a member of the Perseus Books Group
1700 Fourth Street
Berkeley, CA 94710, USA
www.avalontravelbooks.com

Editor: Kevin McLain
Fact checker: Joshua Lawrence Kinser
Copy Editor: Deana Shields
Graphics Coordinator: Domini Dragoone
Production Coordinator: Sean Bellows
Cover Designer: Domini Dragoone
Map Editor: Mike Morgenfeld
Cartographers: Mike Morgenfeld and Kaitlin Jaffe
Proofreader: Danielle Miller
Indexer: Rachel Kuhn

ISBN: 978-1-61238-188-6
ISSN: 2152-3703

Printing History
1st Edition — 2009
2nd Edition — June 2012
5 4 3 2 1